Praise for Andrae D. Smith Jr.

Easy to read and relate to. It is compassionate and detailed in the best ways possible. Love it!

— Barbara Grice, Brand Design Manager
at USA Volleyball

I found myself crying... This book is such a great read and has such a great message that's easy to understand for everyone.

— Avalon Ash, Founder at Alchemy Inc.

Smith's writing style is gentle and honest, refusing to shy away from the reality of being Black in America while inviting the white reader to be compassionate and forgiving with themselves. This message of self-compassion is integral for white Americans to stop feeling uncomfortable when talking about race and is the first step into larger explorations of racism and prejudice.

— Moriah Howell, Managing Editor at
Writer's Digest

Smith's work, *Facing Racism*, is a must-read for white folx, like me, who want to show up with greater self-awareness on their racial justice journey. The combination of critical content and accessible writing style make reading this book feel like you're hanging out with the author, having meaningful conversation over coffee. So good! I highly recommend!

— DR. MOLLIE MONAHAN-KREISHMAN,
FOUNDER OF SOCIAL JUSTICE KIDS

Andrae has a way to touch on difficult topics in a way that does not put you down, but instead gives you awareness to the things you may have not even thought about before. He empowers you to do better and be better. His examples and analogies were easy to follow, with some humor sprinkled in there as well. This is a difficult topic to discuss and Andrae tackled it with extreme class.

— CHRISTINA SNITKO, AUTHOR OF *MIRAGES*

FACING RACISM

ALSO BY ANDRAE D. SMITH JR.

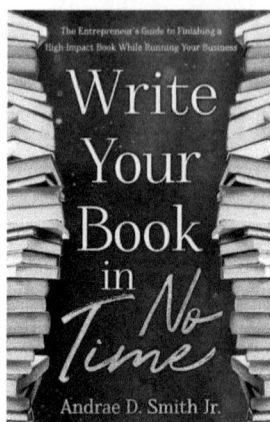

Write Book in No Time

The Entrepreneur's Guide to Finishing a High-impact Book While Running Your Business

FACING RACISM

Overcome Unconscious Bias & Prejudice to Be a Part of the Change

Second Edition

With Foreword by Erin Jones

Andrae D. Smith Jr.

KB
Khrusos Books

DEDICATION

This book is dedicated, first and foremost, to my mother, who worked hard to ensure I had every advantage available to me so that I would not know the sting of racism and prejudice as well as many others have. Thank you for the lessons and endless love.

This book is dedicated, second, to all the mothers out there who've loved children of color and are fighting to protect their futures and create a fairer and more equal world. Thank you.

Third, this book is dedicated to all those who have chosen to stand up against injustice, whose faith in and commitment to true equality and love have prompted them to take action as not only believers but earnest change-makers. Thank you.

This is a book about racism and prejudice.
More than that, it's a book about understanding and empathy.

CONTENTS

FOREWORD

ERIN JONES, AUTHOR OF BRIDGES TO HEAL US

Growing up as one of the only brown people in my neighborhood, I've grappled with the complexities and nuances of race from an early age. My parents, a White couple from Northern Minnesota, adopted me at just three months old, not truly knowing the challenges that adopting a biracial baby would bring them. Through it all, they worked very hard to give my brother and me a better life experience.

When my parents took up teaching jobs at the American School of The Hague, we moved to the Netherlands, where I was fortunate enough to experience many different cultures and people. I moved back to America to attend college at Bryan Mawr, where I realized my story as a biracial international student placed me at the cross-section of many different communities, and I could use my story to start building bridges between them.

Since then, themes like identity, otherness, and belonging have been central in my work. I believe the work of equity and reconciliation starts with sharing our stories as humans and learning to be good listeners. That is one reason why it is my pleasure to write a foreword for *Facing Racism*.

As an educator and avid reader, books have been a constant companion throughout my life. They have been a source of knowl-

edge and inspiration, a window into different perspectives and experiences, and a means of connecting with others. I've read books by
Ibram X Kendi and Dr. Beverly Tatum. I've read the works of Dr.
Brenda Salter-MacNeil, Jemar Tisby, Dr. Martin Luther King, Jr.,
and many more. I have recently added this book to my favorites
because of the way the author uses his story to invite people into the
discussion.

I met Andrae after he published the first edition of this book.
He was introduced to me as someone who could help me write my
own book about racial reconciliation. While writing my book,
Andrae and I witnessed our nation struggle to engage in healthy
ways on issues of race. While some organizations and companies
embraced opportunities to talk about race, others avoided dialogue
at all costs. Andrae is someone who sees people on both sides and
makes space for them.

What I appreciate most about Andrae is that he approaches the
work of racial equity from a life of experience after much self-reflection about his own encounters, struggles, and successes. Andrae
walks his talk. As someone who does racial equity work for a living,
I am exposed to many people with an academic understanding of
the topic but who cannot demonstrate the strategies in person.
Andrae is as gifted and thoughtful in his personal interactions as he
is on paper.

If you're hoping to develop more effective skills for thinking and
talking about race, you will not want to put down this book.
Andrae Smith is a skilled communicator with incredible wisdom
about race, racism, and intercultural communication issues. You
will leave your reading inspired to be on a lifelong journey with
tools and strategies you can employ immediately.

Refusing to shy away from the reality of being Black in America, Andrae invites White readers to be compassionate and forgiving
with themselves as they commit to the self-reflection he models. You
get the sense that he truly cares about people, not just Black or
Brown people, but all people. This book is every bit about making

connections as it is educating, and it is this kind of energy that we need to build braver communities.

I am excited Andrae is re-releasing *Facing Racism*. He is in a new place, personally and professionally, and the world could benefit from exposure to his brilliance. I hope you enjoy this work so much you buy extra copies and share them with those you love to spread the knowledge.

Preface

How could we look at the same event and see two different truths?

When George Floyd was killed in 2020, just months after Ahmaud Arbery, we all watched as one man took his last breath beneath the knee of another. It was primal and traumatic. The world cried together in the face of wanton brutality.

Although we all witnessed the same incident, the aftermath made it clear that (at least in the US) many people saw two unique events. For some, it appeared as "a police officer killing an unarmed suspect." For many of us, it was "another power-tripping white officer taking the law into his own hands to claim another Black life."

What is the truth?

When I published the first edition of *Facing Racism*, my critics (so-called for their opposition rather than literary or academic authority) held the "truth" that I was a racist. They claimed I reduced people to their skin color and exploited a tragedy to push divisive ideologies and construct a false oppressed-and-oppressor worldview. To them, I was just someone who hated America, white people, and myself. Why bother reading books from someone like that? (To be honest, I wouldn't read a book by someone who hates me.) Only... I don't hate them. I don't hate white people, America, or myself (for heaven's sake).

None of that is what this book is about.

I may even be so bold as to say this book isn't even about race. It's about learning to see not truths but the narratives we use to construct our truths.

Long before I ever had the impulse to write a book that would rip me from my comfortable seat in the fantasy genre and plant me firmly in reality, I began studying personal development. From mindfulness meditation to occult alchemy, applied psychology, and human behavior, I read books and bought courses I believed would help me become a better, more mature person and strengthen my character.

These resources taught me many things, but the most valuable takeaway I could have discovered was the concept of the unconscious mind. To think, thoughts govern most of our actions we don't know about in parts of our psyches over which we have no direct control.

It may sound strange at this theoretical level, but the more I worked to understand it, the more I realized some truth in this—in myself and other people. It turns out most people have no idea where their beliefs come from or the stories that control how they experience the world and other people.

Imagine this: You agree that tailgating is a bad driving habit. It is rude and aggressive. You also believe people should not drive the speed limit in the "fast lane." (Note: You should always observe traffic laws in your region.) When someone is driving "slow" in the fast lane, you ride close until they speed up.

When your spouse tells you to stop tailgating, you become upset because it feels like they're calling you a poor driver even though you're not. By definition, you tailgate when you drive closer than the recommended safe driving distance. Still, you don't make the association because you don't see the situation the same way. In your mind, you're not tailgating. The other driver is holding up traffic.

Your spouse saying otherwise feels like an attack because you associate tailgating with bad driving. You know you're not a poor driver, so you can't see yourself having bad driver behaviors.

This is the disconnect I've set out to discuss in this book. Not what is the truth, but how did you come to your version of it?

The problem of prejudice and bias extends well beyond race (especially the history of Black and white people in America). I understand that racism is not just a "Black and white thing." In this country, many communities have experienced prejudice and discrimination based on race, ethnicity, or nationality, which are not represented in this book. Groups such as our Asian, Arabic, Latinx, and Indigenous brothers and sisters have stories I am not equipped to tell.

To this, I ask that you, my reader, please understand that my aim is not to focus on just racial tensions. I've used my experience as an African American to explore concepts like prejudice, discrimination, and bias.

If I had written this book about women, LGBTQ+, Indigenous peoples, Immigrant families, or any other group, the message would have remained the same. On the subject of social change, if you substitute any contentious social issue that seems to be stalled by inaction and debate, the root problem and proposed solution that I explain in chapters 7, 8, and 9 remain the same.

What's different? Why release a second or revised edition of the book?

Typically an author will do so to include significant revisions. The changes I've made are conservative, retaining the core text.

The first notable change is the inclusion of a foreword. I decided to add a foreword because I believed it would help to add perspective on the content and the broader discussion. Social change is community work; many have been leading this work long before I considered lending my voice. One such person is an award-winning educator and speaker, Erin Jones, whose life and efforts are a testament to the heart of my message.

The second major addition is this preface. After *Facing Racism* was first published, it received much praise from readers, but as I noted earlier, it had its critics. While I don't take too much stock of input from people who chose not to read it, I felt it was important to lay out some expectations for this book.

I did not write it for everyone. My intention was that anyone could pick it up and gain value, but I designed it specifically for the white, middle-class Americans who want to see themselves as allies —or at least a part of the solution to a complex problem.

Likewise, it is not an academic or scholarly investigation into racism from historical, psychological, and sociological perspectives. The aim is not to unpack this idea through research and analysis but to open a doorway for people to begin their own personal work and enter the conversation without feeling judged.

Third, in the original text, although I did some research, I did not include any sources, citations, or references. I felt they would be distracting or irrelevant as many people would not do additional research. I've been asked a few times where readers can learn more about a few concepts, and in response, I've included endnotes for some of the more dense or obscure sections.

Each note is a citation to reference material or the link to where the casual reader can find more information. These endnotes do not showcase formal or "scholarly" research but provide context and support as readers move through the core content, so I've not included a formal bibliography.

The fourth major change is the inclusion of two brand-new appendices. The first discusses the brain's method of forming core beliefs and community's role in one's identity and belief. What we see is determined by our beliefs. As new relevant research emerges, I feel it's valuable (though not essential) to know how our communities influence our belief systems.

This is especially important when discussing social change because it impacts how we experience and react to social problems (and if we even see the problems). I gave a brief speech about social change and why I believe personal development is so important to this work. I've included the transcript of the recording. It is connected to the material of this book, but takes a slightly different angle on the conversation. The full video presentation is available on YouTube, and I've included a QR code to for it at the end of the section.

Finally, within the original text, minor typographical errors needed to be addressed. I've also clarified certain examples so that the meaning is not lost or muddled. In a text like this, it is important that the writing is clear and sound so that readers can focus on the message with few distractions. I felt an additional revision would be beneficial.

~

This book, though small, was designed with impact in mind. I feel that no book of its kind is truly complete because there will always be more to discuss. Still, I think this book provides a solid "way in" to a complicated and often uncomfortable conversation.

As you read, I hope you find my stories revealing, personal, relatable, and compassionate. I ask that you remember one thing: we are all responsible for what we create in the world, whether or not we are aware. The first step to creating with intention is realizing how we create.

FACING RACISM

Chapter 1

Ready to Make a Difference?

"John Kennedy believed so strongly that one's aim should not just be the most comfortable life possible, but that we should all do something to right the wrongs we see, and not just complain about them. We owe that to our country, and our country will suffer if we don't serve her. He believed that one man can make a difference—and that every man should try."
— Jacqueline Kennedy

It was 9:15 at night, and I was sitting in bed reading a book about a girl who follows a white rabbit down an unusually long tunnel (because you're never too old for an adventure in Wonderland). *Bzzzt.* My phone vibrated on the nightstand next to me: a new text message from Allison.

"Hey... How are you? I'm so sorry for what's happening to Black people in this country. I just wanted to let you know I stand with you. <3"

Clearly, she'd been watching the news. Another unarmed Black man was killed by a white police officer, and people nationwide were furious. The video of what happened had been circulating the internet for days, and it was pretty traumatizing. Hard to imagine anyone could be so... so... *evil*, yeah, that's the right word.

Of course, this was not the first time an unarmed black man or woman had been murdered by law enforcement, but this was the first time any of my non-Black friends had ever sent me a message like this. As I started typing my response to express how much the text meant to me, two new messages popped onto my screen, back-to-back.

Jen wrote, "Hi Andrae. Are you okay? These are crazy times. I wish I knew what to say right now but I'm too shocked and heart-broken. I love you."

Nathan wrote, "Hey man, I just wanted to check on you. I know I can never understand what it's like to be you and live with racism every day, but I hope you know I'm against it and will do what I can to support change. Stay safe."

Okay. Something was definitely different this time. Maybe it's the way the media was covering the story. Maybe it's the way #BlackLivesMatter (yes, that again) had overrun the internet with desperate, frustrated cries for justice and change. Maybe it's the way the video showed undeniable proof that something is disparagingly wrong with the status quo. Whatever the reason, it looks like white Americans were just as shaken by this as the Black community, and they couldn't sit by and do nothing. Not this time.

Now, I'd be doing my friends a huge disservice if I didn't point out that they're all genuinely good people. The fact that this was the first time any of them had messaged me regarding racial injustice doesn't mean they've ever consciously supported racism. To be honest, racism probably doesn't even cross their minds most of the time. Each of them, in their own way, is the average American: kind, hardworking, just trying to make a living Monday through Friday and enjoy their lives Saturday and Sunday.

I bet if you'd asked any of them what they thought about racism on any given day up 'til this night, they'd all agree it's a good thing slavery is illegal and things are more equal now. (I mean, Black people are making literally millions of dollars in sports and enter-tainment and we've had our first Black President. Things are *way* better than they used to be. *Right?*)

And besides, Jen's sisters all dated or married Black men, and Nathan's stepson is mixed. Plus, they all have at least one Black friend (me). It wouldn't make sense to think they had a problem with people of color.

So, what changed?

I did reply to each of them that night, expressing my gratitude and reassuring them that I didn't think badly of them at all. I mean, how could I? What happened wasn't their fault. They had nothing to do with it, but they still thought about me and felt compelled to reach out. That should be proof of the type of people they are.

The truth is, up until that point, they never really had to think about racism. Most of their friends and family are white or "successful" Black people like me. They felt ashamed that it had existed right in front of them for so long, but because they aren't racist—at least not consciously—it always felt so distant. They felt angry that it took seeing another man losing his life for them to realize the problem wasn't getting "fixed." They felt scared for the future of the country and their families if something didn't change fast, and while they weren't quite sure what to do, they knew it was time to step up and be a part of the solution somehow.

I found Nathan's last message incredibly moving. He said, "It makes me mad thinking that my kids might have to deal with this when they get older. My son is losing friends because of this, and it's not fair. As a parent, I have to do what I can to give all my kids the best future possible and I'll be damned if I lose any of mine to a coward with a badge."

If you've picked up this book, it's safe to assume you, like my friends above, have come face-to-face with a moral urge to take a stand against injustice directed at minorities and people of color. Whether it's because you have friends or relatives who fall into that demographic or you're fed up with of watching people get murdered without justice or you believe in upholding the ideals of our country, you have found a reason to look this problem in the face and say, "Not one more."

Likewise, it's safe to assume that, though you've agreed to take up the calling, you're not sure of exactly what you can do to make a difference—or if you even *can*. Well, to echo the quote from our former First Lady that I opened the chapter with, "One man [you] can make a difference and [you] should try." I'm a firm believer that change is not made by a few great people doing remarkable things, but by the sum of many passionate people lovingly doing what they can.

That being said, you're in the right place at the right time. You wouldn't be reading this book right now if you didn't believe at some level that you *can* make a difference. As you progress through its pages, you will come to know what racism is, where it comes from, what you can do right now to actively resist it, and, most importantly, the key to creating lasting change for a brighter future.

In the next chapter, you'll get to know who I am, how I came to discover my solution, and why I know it works. If you're serious about making the world a better, safer place—and I'm sure you are —then keep reading.

REFLECTIONS

Take a moment and think about why you have decided to read this book. Why have you chosen to engage in this work now? What difference do you hope to make? What would success look like to you and how will you know you've achieved it? Feel free to use the space below or a separate journal to write down your thoughts.

Chapter 2

It Could Have Been Me

"I have a dream that my four children will one day live in a nation where they will not be judged by the color of their skin, but by the content of their character."
— Dr. Martin Luther King Jr.

I remember sometime between December 2011 and January 2012, I was having a fight with my mom—one of many that year. It was the middle of my senior year, and I hadn't yet turned eighteen, so you can imagine I was still stubborn and headstrong. That's right, I was not always the calm and compassionate person who's writing this book for you now! I was by no means the picture of a "troubled teen," but as a star athlete with a 4.26 GPA, it wouldn't be a stretch to say I thought I had the world figured out (the tell-tale signs of one who knows nothing).

I was about to go out for a run that evening and had just put on my track uniform: black sweatpants with a white stripe down the side, a pair of dusty gray running shoes (Asics), and a black hoodie with my school logo printed in white and gold on the front. As I approached the front door, my mom stopped me.

"Don't go out in that," she said.

"Why not? It's my school uniform," I replied indignantly.

"I don't like the way it looks."

"Mom, it's my school uniform." Sensing where she was going, I added, "Nothing's going to happen if I go out for a jog. I'm going to Redlands where it's safer anyway."

At the time, I lived in San Bernardino, California—a city that was clean and safe once upon a time when Norton Air Force Base was operating but had slowly devolved into one of Cali's most dangerous cities (even beating out places like Los Angeles, Compton, and Oakland at times). Oddly enough, just a twelve-minute drive south, the city of Redlands boasted the most millionaires per capita in the region and was generally considered cleaner, safer, and a better place to raise a family. That's also where I went to school. So, I had no worries about jogging in my obvious school sweats in a nicer (predominately white) neighborhood.

"Dionne," she said.

Ugh! My middle name.

"Don't. Wear. It." Her voice was low, and she spoke slowly and deliberately, annunciating every letter the way she did when she really wasn't playing games.

"I'll. Be. Fine." I said, mimicking her style.

You can probably guess what came next. A little disbelief on her part, some more stubbornness on mine, something about fixing my tone, and, of course, the classic line, "Why don't you make me?!" Needless to say, teenage Andrae did *not* go jogging that evening. Nor did he go anywhere at all that week. Eventually, we got over it, and I agreed not to go jogging in all black like that. Instead, we bought some brightly colored, very obvious workout gear so it was clear that I was just a high school kid out for some exercise.

Fast forward to early March 2012. The news stations were starting to blow up with sketches of some dark-skinned kid in a hoodie. I never really listened to the news other than to catch what the weather was going to do. When I saw the image, I assumed they were reporting on a Black teen suspected of some act of delinquency, as was the usual report for my area, and wrote it off.

I found out quickly that I was wrong. It was Trayvon Martin

(age seventeen), a Black boy in my age range, killed while walking home from the corner store with a pack of Skittles and a Mountain Dew. He was wearing his hood up and happened to be seen by an over-zealous neighborhood watchman with a gun, George Zimmerman. On February 26, 2012—weeks after my fight with my mom—Trayvon Martin was shot dead because he was in the wrong place at the wrong time with the wrong look...

Trayvon Martin at Age 17

This incident rocked the nation and sparked the Black Lives Matter movement, as we all know. But me? Personally, I was "shook." Not only was mom right (*whaaa?*), but this was the first time in *my* life when racism seemed real and dangerous.

Now, I wasn't stupid. I knew racism wasn't gone in America, but something about seeing a teenage boy's face on the screen and realizing that it could have easily been me or one of my classmates changed things for me. I could have *been* him. Racism went from being something that was dying off slowly as people became better-educated to something that *needed* to be eradicated swiftly and decisively. Surely, the man who shot down a child would be convicted.

Me at Age 17

The course of the trial revealed a lot of things to me that year. Remember how I said I went to school in Redlands? Imagine my surprise when I realized that I had white friends who didn't believe Zimmerman was guilty, friends who, even though he shot a teenager after being told not to engage, believed that he "did what he had to do." Imagine my surprise to hear people I ate lunch with and played sports with, people I high-fived in the locker room and tutored in the library, say things like, "Well, he wouldn't have gotten shot if he had just listened" and "I don't think we're getting the whole story. The news says Trayvon might have been involved with drugs and gangs." (As if not listening to a strange man with a gun or having an *allegedly* disreputable past as a teenager was enough to justify getting shot and killed.)

Believe me, I was pissed. I felt a deep anger and sense of betrayal. How could *my* friends not care about someone who looked like me and my other Black classmates? And how could these same friends speak so insensitively and still want to hang out? To me, it was obvious racism, but they just didn't see it.

Now, it would paint an unfair picture of the town if I suggested from this that Redlands is racist—at least in the sense that they approve of hate speech and violence and discrimination. It's a genuinely good town, with well-intentioned people who probably aren't aware of underlying prejudices. I did also have many white classmates (and teachers!) who sympathized and knew that something about what had happened was obviously wrong. It was with them that I learned the foundation for what would turn into the information outlined in this book. These people understood something critical that the others didn't.

One day, my best friend and I were hanging out in our favorite teacher's classroom during lunch. Everyone was out playing touch football, so it was just us. The trial was still going so I asked him how he thought it would end. Before we knew where we were headed, I went into a full rant about how mad I was and why it was getting hard to keep liking white people. He cut me off after a minute.

He always had this calmness about him when he talked. It was like an anchor for people to latch onto when they needed to come back down to earth a little. Clearly, I was getting lost, so he looked me in the eyes and spoke, slowly at first.

"Dude... You know what I think? I think you're right to be mad, but you shouldn't hate white people. Hating them just gives them more reason to hate you back. You know? Instead of hating each other over differences, we should focus on what we have in common. At the core, we all have the same basic needs. We're more alike than we are different."

"It's not their differences I hate," I said, "it's their behavior."

What he said next, I hope I never forget. He said, "Yeah, but remember people only act a certain way because it's how they were taught. It's easy to blame other people when we think they're wrong, but just think, if they really knew better, they would do better. Prejudice and hatred only come from lack of understanding."

Just like that, the anger I was feeling in that moment was gone. He was right. Hatred and prejudice are a byproduct of ignorance, and if there was one thing I wouldn't be, it was ignorant. If I really thought about it, none of my friends had turned on me or treated me any differently. This showed me that, at the very least, they didn't know how hateful they sounded, and because of how they were raised, they wouldn't get it if I explained it to them.

Over time, the conversations I was having changed from heated debates to challenging and personal discussions where people didn't feel judged. That feeling of security is what allowed for new ideas to come up, whereas before, conversations would start to shut down in frustration. What I had learned and would consequently go on to master was that in allowing myself to truly see other people, I opened a window through which I, too, could be seen. That made all of the difference when it came to having productive communication about tough subjects like racism.

Of course, at eighteen years old, I didn't learn all of the skills and dexterity I'd need in order to successfully navigate such a rough terrain as human emotions, social conditioning, and subconscious bias—all of which must be addressed if we are to even discuss the issue of racism. Still, I had found a lantern to see what was coming up ahead of me. In the next chapter, you will learn to see this book as your lantern, shedding light on the path as you strive toward understanding, identifying, and confronting racism for yourself.

REFLECTIONS

Do you remember where you were when you first heard about the Trayvon Martin case? How did it make you feel? How did people around you respond? Would your reactions be the same if it happened today, and if not, what has changed? Feel free to use the space below or a separate journal to write down your thoughts.

CHAPTER 3

A BETTER WAY

"Lasting social change unfolds from inside out: from the inner to the
outer being, from inner to outer realities."
— Arianna Huffington

In the years since we lost Trayvon, we've seen many more high-profile cases of unarmed Black Americans being killed by police officers. Eric Garner (2014), Michael Brown (2014), Tamir Rice (2014), Walter Scott (2015), Philando Castile (2016), Stephen Clark (2018), Elijah McClain (2019), Breonna Taylor (2020), and George Floyd (2020)—to name just a few. I won't go into the details of their cases here because I believe you're capable of digging deeper on your own, and I don't want to color your experience of the information. For now, we can focus on the impact these cases had on my understanding of racism.

When many of these incidents occurred, I was living in Colorado Springs and building my career as a department manager at a prominent retail chain where I would come to learn so much more about understanding people. You see, Colorado Springs is a pleasant city, regarded as one of the best and fastest-growing cities in the nation due to its largely military and retiree population. It's safe, affordable, and great for families. Situated near the southern range of the Colorado Rockies, it's also loaded with beautiful views if you love hiking and nature. But there is one thing you should also know...

Colorado is not known for its diverse demographics. I'm reminded of a video I saw online years ago that captures the idea—albeit in a humorous and slightly facetious way. A Black man set up a booth at a local festival in Aspen, and his sign read, "Meet a Black guy!" Over the course of this video, I watched many friendly and well-meaning white folks rush up to him like children, eager to shake his hand and take a picture with him, like they'd never seen someone of color before. And perhaps they *hadn't*. At any rate, the man made a few bucks, and we all got a laugh at how homogeneous that community was. (Imagine my surprise when I realized that Aspen was only a few hours north of me.)

Knowing this, you would be right in assuming our store's demographic was similar. I was one of just a few African Americans, and one of only two or three Black supervisors in a store of 300 employees. So, as these incidents took over the news, the breakroom was abuzz time and again with chatter—often about how sad it was... that the media was pushing an anti-police agenda and "trying to start another race war." (Really? People were dead and they were worried about how it *looked* on the news?)

Now, since I spent an average of ten hours a day with these people, I knew they weren't bad people. The sporting goods manager was always good for conversation about outdoor adventure and the latest sports equipment. Old Man Jim, the automotive manager, was quiet but always sure to say, "Good morning" as he passed me in the back hallway carrying his paper cup of black coffee. Dani was a devoted mom of two rowdy boys. She also had a thing for darker skin and muscles. And Janice was the grandmother you'd imagine when people talk about baking cookies and telling stories at Christmas time. Nope, I wouldn't have pegged any of them for racists.

But there they were, clearly (as I saw it) disregarding the loss of human life and writing off news coverage as "liberal bias." It was like my experience in high school all over again. Still, they were my friends and colleagues. If I was going to keep building my career, I would have to be able to quell my own frustrations, ignore every impulse I had to "set the record straight," and focus on one goal: maintaining good workplace relationships. After all, they were just different, not hateful. I was also sure that avoiding the conversations wouldn't make a difference.

It was in having these tough conversations with people who thought differently that I mastered the skill that has been so instrumental in dealing with prejudice whenever I've encountered it. If you're eager to know just what this skill is and can't imagine waiting to find out, I will tell you. But don't be surprised if it seems obvious.

The skill that's been the key to unlocking and overcoming prejudice is *empathy*.

In psychological terms, empathy is defined as "understanding another person's experience by imagining oneself in that other person's situation. One understands the other person's experience as if it were being experienced by the self, but without the self actually experiencing it."[1]

Fundamentally, this is the same concept my best friend described that day in the classroom. Empathy is the tool by which we bypass our usual experience or perspective regarding a given situation and come to understand it through someone else's eyes. It's the whole "walking a mile in the other person's shoes" adage put into practice.

Now, while that may sound simple, truly putting empathy into practice is anything but. And when it comes to combating prejudice and dismantling racism, most of us don't even notice when we're not being empathetic. It's also only half of the equation. Empathy without *action* accomplishes very little. We'll dive deeper into this in chapter 9.

Since you've committed to taking a stance and making a positive change in your sphere of influence, I've committed to helping you do the work. Therefore, the process which I'm about to outline for you here is designed to take you through ten critical steps that will allow you to get started easily from where you are right now. But before I do, there is just one more thing you should know.

In the course of the book, we will be exploring, in brief, the mechanics of racism, the psychology of prejudice, and the narratives that make people think and behave the way they do.

I would ask that you approach each topic and discussion with an open mind and with patience, not only with the material but with the things that may come up for you. This process may bring up feelings like anger, sorrow, guilt, or shame. You may feel triggered. Know that *all* of the things that come up for you are *totally* valid. You needn't feel judged for them. Likewise, if some of the information doesn't "click" right away, you needn't feel bad. You're not failing nor are you a bad person for not fully grasping some things that come up. The fact that you're reading this book shows me that your heart is in the right place. So, I invite you to keep reading, and we'll get through this together.

WHAT'S IN THIS BOOK?

Below is a basic rundown of the steps involved in the work ahead and what to expect in each:

In chapter 4, you'll learn to see today's struggles with racism not as new or re-occurrence but as part of our ongoing narrative of our shared American history. You'll also understand why it is so important to turn off your unconscious "guilt" triggers so you can proceed with the essential work of this and start to make a difference.

In chapter 5, you'll learn to recognize common ways in which racism and prejudice have infiltrated our daily life socially and institutionally, as well as the danger that comes with allowing these things to remain invisible in our modern world.

In chapter 6, you'll learn what white privilege is and how it's possible to be privileged and not see it. They will also learn the difference between *equality* and *equity* and why the latter is more necessary right now.

In chapter 7, we start mining at the core of the problem. I'll show how societal racism is actually a result of unconscious bias and prejudice by giving you a basic understanding of the shadow self and how it impacts your beliefs and behaviors. After reading this chapter, you'll have an approachable framework for uncovering what's in your shadow and how to deprogram it so that you can consciously counter any prejudice you find within yourself and challenge it when you see it in others.

In chapter 8, we start dissolving the illusion of separation that allows racial prejudice to persist. You'll develop an entry-level grasp of the cognitive process of *otherization* and how it has created the racist environment we see today.

In chapter 9, we'll explore empathy at a much deeper level. You'll understand what it is, what it looks and feels like, how to apply it, and why it's vital to confronting racism in ourselves and each other. You'll see how mastering and modeling empathy is the only way to truly build connections and bring communities together.

In chapter 10, I'll show you five valuable skills to help you navigate the uncomfortable conversations you're bound to have with grace and courage. You'll see how each technique or pillar of a courageous conversation will allow you to communicate in ways that support progressive conversation without causing a sense of isolation.

In chapter 11, you'll learn four easy ways to start doing anti-racism work in your own sphere and start making a difference right away. After working through the previous chapters, you'll have the essential skills to understand the impact and responsibility you have, as well as the confidence to act on what you'll know by the end of this book.

Once again, this is only a brief overview, a sample of what's in store for us. These steps are ordered in a way that is meant to be easy to follow and integrate, like wading into the pool instead of cannon-balling right into the deep end. In the next chapter, we'll be getting our feet wet by exploring how we got to where we are now.

REFLECTIONS

Think about the communities you're a part of. Is there much racial, ethnic, or ideological diversity? Do the voices present represent different lived experiences? Are the people in your social groups open to hearing the experiences of others? If not, where are the spaces where you can hear from people with different worldviews? Feel free to use the space below or a separate journal to write down your thoughts.

CHAPTER 4

HOW DID WE GET HERE?

"People are trapped in history and history is trapped in them."
— James Baldwin

So, do you remember the text message I got from my friend Allison at the beginning of chapter 1? Well, like I said, I replied, expressing my sincerest gratitude for her thinking of me. We ended up texting back and forth for a little while that night, talking about what had happened, how wrong it was that anyone could do something so horrible, and how she couldn't imagine living with fear every day. Hell, she really *got* it. She was seeing, perhaps for the first time in her life, the dark side of things.

I texted her back, "Well, this sort of thing happens too often to be afraid. It's like rain in summer. There's always a chance, but where you live makes the difference."

She replied, "That's true. I don't know how you're always so optimistic. I'm kinda scared because it seems like it's getting worse. It's happening too much now."

This made me pause. *It's happening too much... now?* Was it not too much before? I was itching to ask her what she meant, to call her out a little bit. I mean, really, if you knew anything about American history, you know that Black people getting killed has been an ongoing narrative since the first slave ships landed Virginia. This is what the whole Civil Rights movement was about in the last century, and even then, we've still had violence and prejudice against African Americans at the hands of those in law enforcement.

Of course, I refrained from typing and shook off my momentary disbelief. It wasn't her fault. For one thing, her family immigrated from Europe when she was younger, so her understanding of US history was understandably limited. The other thing I had to remember was that the extent of Black history taught in our school system covered just a few things:

- Trans-Atlantic slave trade
- American slavery and the Civil War
- Segregation and Jim Crow laws
- Civil Rights activist like Rosa Parks, Dr. Martin Luther King, and (briefly) Malcolm X and the Black Panther Party

No class I took talked about the positive contributions of Black Americans, such as jazz and rock music or inventions like traffic lights and the popular "monkey" wrench (so-called in insult to the inventor, Jack Johnson).[1] No class talked about how Black Americans served in both World Wars, pioneering such decorated divisions as the Tuskegee Airmen, but were denied VA rights here at home. No class ever mentioned Emmett Till or Rodney King—except to point out that the ensuing "race" riots were the worst in American history. And of course, before the internet explosion of the 2010s, there was no way to capture and broadcast police brutality or abuse of power en masse like there is today.

So, it would be no understatement to say she just didn't know any better, not the way I would, having Black parents and grandparents who've lived through it all. Like my other high school friends and former coworkers, her perspective was severely limited by her lack of adequate information.

While planning this book, I went back and forth a few times, trying to decide on exactly where to start our journey. Clearly, I wanted to get to the heart of the matter right away and teach you how to start confronting racism in everyday life. However, if the conversation highlighted above is any evidence, the obvious place to start is clearing up two major misconceptions about racism in our society. The first is that this is something new and that you are directly responsible for creating it. Let's take a closer look.

This Is Nothing New – Understand the Story to Break the Curse

The problems we face today are not new but inherited from generations of trauma and division handed down directly and indirectly for the last 400 years. The fight we're having now started long ago and permeates every layer of our culture and psychology like a generational curse that we must end. And while I don't have the space in this book to cover the volumes it would take to discuss the racial history of America thoroughly, what I would like to do now is look at a piece of the story of how we got here as it pertains to you and me.

On May 25, 2020, the entire world witnessed the merciless and intentional murder of George Floyd. Amid the outrage and heartache, many have asked the inevitable question: What would make these officers—or any human being in civilized society—think that this would be acceptable? Sadly, the answer is precedent. You saw the list of names in the previous chapter. Many of the officers in those cases were not charged, and they are not alone. America has a history of killing unarmed Black Americans.

1992: The "LA Race Riots"

Also called the Rodney King Riots, this violent outcry was not a mere eruption of racial tensions, but the public response when the officers who beat King were acquitted in court. Rodney King was an LA man who was under arrest following a high-speed when four officers brutally assaulted him, beating him half to death. What was the Civil Rights movement for if gangsters in badges could literally get away with obvious attempted murder? Weren't cops supposed to be the good guys and protect people and stop crime? Yeah, sure, if you're on the white side of history.

Police forces in many states (but especially in the South, where slavery had a bigger impact on the economy) had originated as privately funded Slave Patrol. Their entire purpose was to capture runaway slaves, and later, in the Jim Crow Era, to keep the Blacks in line. Sure, the cops were there to protect and serve, but their service has always been to the white community, to which Black people have always been "the bad guy."

This brings up another major point, which is that modern discussions of Jim Crow treat it like it was too far off in history to be relevant and like it wasn't *that* bad. Make no mistake, these American Dark Ages defined what it meant to be Black in America for nearly one hundred years (1865-ish to 1964). It was a period of *legal* discrimination that went far deeper than "whites only" pools and restaurants. If you looked like me in this time period, you would be reminded unequivocally that you were not equal to a white person. Period.

It meant that you could not be paid equally. You could not vote in many places. You could have your home vandalized and destroyed and be barred from purchasing a new home. If a white person was insulted by your sneeze, you could be beaten with no legal consequences. In fact, going to the police station might have gotten you or your family killed. And the fight to end this lasted until nearly the 1970s! Ending this was the purpose of the Civil Rights movement.

To say that racism is over or that there is no more racism would be to pretend we could possibly overturn 350 years' worth of psychological and systemic dehumanization of the Black American in just 50 years. To suggest that today's incidents and protests are new or outlier behavior in this modernized nation neglects the truth, that we've been saying, "Black lives matter" for 150 years. Only back then, it looked a lot more like "all lives" as Black people worked to hold the nation accountable to its pledge of "liberty and justice *for all*." (You'd think, after so much time, we'd have a more inclusive definition for the word "all.")

All of that is to shatter any misconceptions that the "race problem" we're discussing is just coming up "all of a sudden"—that it wasn't a problem until Black people started talking about it in the last decade. Our racial history created the world we live in today. It's been woven into the very fabric of our American life, from clothes and music and language to politics and economics.

If you trace back the evolution of Black culture, you won't find a reclaiming of African roots (those were lost at sea and beaten out of us with Bibles and whips), but rather a progression of Black responses to white America's macro and micro-aggressions. You'll see attempt after attempt at claiming dignity, recognition, and something to call our own as a people who were no longer welcome but had no home to claim. As the latest generation to join the racial discussion, this (racism) is our inheritance.

As a brief illustration, I'd like you to consider this metaphor: You're a painter like your parents before you and theirs before them. Your grandfather hands down his old brush to your father, who hands it to you. So, now it is yours. They're proud of it, despite it being an antiquated tool that's missing bristles in the middle, causing every stroke to leave a gap or light spot in the middle. You've become proficient at painting over those flaws, but the problem still exists and prevents you from painting certain strokes. It's getting increasingly difficult to keep up with new art styles. At some point, it makes sense to say, "This brush is crap! It may have worked for Dad and Grandpa, but I'm getting a new one. Even if it means I have to spend a little extra money and take time learning new painting habits. I can't paint the pictures I want to with this old brush."

Just like the painter aspires to paint a fresh, new picture and needs to let go of the ineffective tool he's inherited, so must we let go of the things that have been passed on to us—which requires some difficult work beyond "loving all people." Loving everyone equally is good (that's the goal!), but the things that must be faced are subconscious biases and predispositions. These are stigmas like being nervous to date outside your race because your family wouldn't understand or assuming you'll get better service from a business owner who looks like you because he's somehow more likely to be fair and professional. These are emotions, attitudes, and triggers that may not make sense—that we may not even see—like becoming fearful when around people of color. These are systematic practices that exclude and divide and have become normalized, like whites and Blacks being charged differently for the same crimes.

It's more important now than ever for each of us to lean into the work of understanding, identifying, and challenging racism, both in ourselves and in our institutions. The world we're in is not our own, and if we ever hope to hand off a better one, we have to leave this one in the past—never forgetting but agreeing to move forward from it.

YOU DIDN'T CREATE THE PROBLEM – BUT YOU DECIDE WHERE IT GOES FROM HERE

Knowing what we've covered above, you may be feeling a little shame or guilt for not seeing this before. You might even feel like this is somehow your fault. And it's not hard to see why. The internet is loaded with cries of "If you do nothing, then this is your fault!" And that's what's stirred you to become a part of the solution. Right?

The other misconception I feel it's important to address from the outset is the notion that you are responsible for creating the world today and that you need to apologize for what your ancestors did. We all know you did not create this problem. It's true that you could have done more to learn about and confront racism a long time ago. It's true the information's been out there. But couldn't it also be true that you grew up with a heritage that did actually address the race problem?

This is one of the most important takeaways from this chapter because, as I'll explain in detail later, when we feel guilt or shame, the natural response is to reject the things that make us feel that way. It's the same mechanism that makes children blame others for things they did in order to avoid getting in trouble. It's imperative that you're able to avoid that pitfall. In order to do the work that comes in the later chapters and actually achieve our shared goal, you'll have to come face-to-face with *your* direct and indirect impact on racism in the modern world. You won't be able to do that if your brain is telling you to run because it makes you feel bad.

This does not absolve you of your role in perpetuating or eliminating racism in society today. For instance, consider some of these common rebuttals to Black Lives Matter: "All lives matter," "Rioting is wrong," "Not all police are bad," and "You can't blame all white people for the actions of a few." These are all true statements, and you may have said some of them yourself. On their own, these comments would be innocuous, but I want to be perfectly clear, the people who are saying them in response to Black Lives Matter are doing little more than giving themselves a reason to not get involved. The existence of racism is so ugly and inconvenient to have to deal with, it's easier to deflect to simple statements like this. It's like saying, "Well, if Black people would just remember that we all matter, we wouldn't have to talk about race," which is a convenient way to sweep racists and racism under the rug and pretend they don't exist.

Understand, the goal of this book—of the activism happening in the country—is not to make you feel like a racist and fall into a fit of self-pity but to get you to call out real racists and racism wherever they exist. By acknowledging that this history and these micro-aggressions exist for all of us and that you did not directly create them, you allow yourself to stop feeling guilty and to keep leaning in so that you can own your role in co-creating a better reality for the next generation.

That said, you need to forgive yourself for not knowing what you didn't know (bet you didn't think this was *that* kind of book, eh?) so that you can get comfortable learning uncomfortable truths about our society and even yourself. That may be hard now, but that's okay. For now, I want you to practice internalizing the following mantra by saying it every time you start to feel uncomfortable about a topic pertaining to racism:

"The problems we're facing in this world didn't start with me, but I have the power to change things. I don't have to be perfect, but I'm committed to learning and growing, even when it's hard."

This applies to both the world around us and, to some extent, the world within us. (Again, I'll be explaining this in a later chapter.) As we proceed, hold onto that thought. If you start to feel anxious or like you can't move forward, come back to it, and remember that you can take responsibility without blaming yourself. You and I both know you're not a bad person. Like I said before, you wouldn't be here if you didn't care, which shows you are ready.

That being said, I realize this chapter has been really intense for you. I feel it too. Before moving on to the next chapter, I would like to invite you to do a short meditation to loosen up any tight energy:

Get seated comfortably with your feet planted flat on the floor. If you prefer to lie down, that is 100 percent okay too. Next, take five deep breaths, pulling the air deep into your belly and then emptying your lungs completely. Once you've done that, bring your attention to the soles of your feet. What do you feel? Is there any sensation? Any tightness? If so, give it permission to relax, releasing whatever tension you can with a gentle exhale, not forcing, not trying. Bring your attention up your body (calves, knees, hips, glutes, abdomen, back, etc.) until you reach the top of your head. Once you've done that, say the following out loud or in your head, "I'm aware of my body and the excess tension I've been carrying. I let it go now and feel ready to move forward."

Good. You should be ready to continue. In the next chapter, we'll be looking at how racism shows up in our world today.

Reflections

What has been your experience learning about or discussing racism or African American History? How do you feel things might be different if we had more transparent education about America's relationship with race?

CHAPTER 5

WHAT DOES RACISM LOOK LIKE TODAY?

"It would be interesting to find out what goes on in that moment when someone looks at you and draws all sorts of conclusions."
— Malcolm Gladwell

Now that we've talked about some of the history of racism in our society, you should have a beginner-level understanding of the way that it's changed faces over the decades. Next, we need to spend some time going over some ways in which racism presents itself for us today so that we can know what it is we're actually looking for.

In regular usage, the word "racism" basically describes the belief that personal qualities such as ideals, morals, and behaviors are connected to race and the belief that one race is inherently superior to others. In this context, a racist is someone who believes that they are superior to an entire group of people based on attributes connected with their race. This is a pretty good definition for everyday use. Still, I'd actually like to propose an alternate definition from a sociological perspective that, for our purposes, may be more specific and useful.

In sociology, racism at its core is more than a superiority complex; it creates an imbalance of power or opportunity between people along racial lines and is the *active* result of prejudice. Put another way, it promotes a society's "dominant" racial group and allows them to create structures and institutions that reinforce their beliefs. The common use of the word "racism," though moderately accurate, is more akin to racial prejudice, which only refers to harboring unsubstantiated (often negative) beliefs about another group based on race. It doesn't take into account the systemic inequality that arises with the prejudice. From this point on, when you see any of the words above used in this book, you can assume that I'm using them in this context.

If you're wondering how you're supposed to keep track of this, don't worry! There is no pop quiz at the end of this chapter. You won't need to remember the exact definitions in order to make changes. I gave them to you here mainly to get us speaking the same language. The only thing you have to take from the information above is this: prejudice is the part of the problem that deals with personal beliefs (which can be conscious or subconscious), and racism is the part of the problem that deals with social order—it's a mechanism that employs racial discrimination to act on and reinforce prejudicial attitudes within society.

Now, keep in mind that I've simplified this as much as possible for you because the full breakdown would be well beyond the scope of this book. So, even though these are the definitions *I'm* using, sociologists and experts on racism will tell you this excludes a lot of information. For now, my focus is just to provide us with a working language. The other thing I want to make clear here is that racism in America and even around the world *is* a deep and complex subject that I can't possibly cover in just this one book. To fully understand how deep it runs, you could probably read three encyclopedias, and that doesn't include racism toward Latinos, Asians, Arabs, or Indians. Our focus in this book is aimed at understanding prejudice (the personal level) and transmuting it into opportunities for growth that can be put into practice right now, and hopefully open the door to more intense conversations.

So, getting back to the focus of this chapter, how do prejudice and racism appear in the world today? How can you recognize them when you see them? Well, it can be as innocuous as common stereo-types—you know, the kind we all joke about. Stop me if you've heard these:

- Black guys are good at playing basketball
- Black people love fried chicken and watermelon
- white people can't dance
- white people don't season food
- Asians are good at math

These are a harmless type of prejudice that, nevertheless, create implicit impressions about members of these racial groups. And they come up almost without much thought. For instance, let's say you're white, and your Black friend invites you to have Thanks-giving dinner with his family. You would hate to show up empty-handed, so you ask what you should bring. After thinking for a minute, he says, "You know, you can bring some soda. No way you can mess that up." (Obviously, suggesting your food would be bland.) Now, since you guys have been friends for a while, you say, "Okay. Should I get orange or grape?" (Because Black folks love orange and grape soda, right?)

You see? Harmless! But what if this wasn't your close friend? What if it was a coworker you were getting to know? Can you say that some part of you wouldn't be at least *a little* offended by his comment on your cooking? He's never tried your food. He made an assumption based on your racial identity. And can you say with absolute certainty that your "orange or grape" comeback would have been seen as a tasteful joke?

This sort of stereotyping, though commonplace, is a form of prejudice that can prove more harmful if we're not careful. In fact, this reminds me of a conversation I had with some of my high school classmates. Back then, I was the video production manager for the football team, so I spent a lot of time with these guys after school.

One afternoon, I was walking from the boy's locker room with some of the guys after practice. They were talking about all things teenage boys talk about, like lifting weights, their junk size, and of course, the girls they thought were H. O. T. As usual, I was pretty quiet. It wasn't that I didn't have an opinion on any of these things, but I had to keep up my "cool guy" image. Kids back then looked at me like I was in a world of my own because I got better grades, could out-lift most of them in the weight room, wore nice clothes and dark shades, and had a pretty sister with pretty girl friends.

Naturally, though, the questions had to come. One of the guys spoke up and asked, "Hey Drae, who do you like? You do like girls, right?"

"Dude! Don't ask Drae that," said another. "Of course he likes girls."

"I'm just asking because he never talks about anyone," said the first guy. "His sister's got cute friends."

"Duh, but he can't hit on his sister's friends. Right, Drae?"

"Exactly," I said.

"Nah, I know what it is," said the fourth guy in our group. "Drae's not into Black girls."

Really? I thought. Did he not see my sun-kissed skin? "Dude, really?" I said.

The first guy chimed in, "I think you're right. Drae's Black, but not *Black-Black.*"

The fourth guy said, "Yeah, Drae, you're pretty white. You don't act all ghetto like other Black people. You're quiet and smart. Not loud like those girls."

"Yep," said the second guy. (Wasn't he on my side a second ago?) "Drae's too smart for Black girls."

I couldn't believe what I was hearing. I mean, somehow to them, my intelligence and quiet demeanor made me too good for my own people. They may not have realized it then, but what they were really saying was that Black girls aren't smart, that Black girls are loud and ghetto. They were saying that because I didn't act

Black (meaning I was more like a white person somehow), Black girls weren't good enough for me.

Clearly, they were watching too much MTV or something. The media image of Black women is loud, undereducated, and a little mean (something we'll have to continue working to change), and for these teenage boys, that image created a bias which they tried to project onto me. Believe it or not, African American women hold more college degrees than African American men do. So, to even suggest that I was too smart for Black girls was unfounded. But that's the beauty of prejudice and stereotypes.

This is still a fairly harmless instance in the grand scheme of things. Do you remember the fight I had with my mom in chapter 2 about me wearing a black hoodie to go jogging? My mom was afraid that if I went jogging dressed like that, I might get "mistaken" for a hoodlum or Black delinquent looking for trouble in a neighborhood that I had no business in.

I didn't think I would have been in any real danger then, but as I reflect on that night now, I can't help but wonder what if someone had seen me in the wrong light that night, if someone whose only image of Black teenagers in hoods was as gangsters or drug dealers or vandals had seen me and called the police with their suspicions? I wonder if any officers responding to the call would have recognized that I was just a student at the town's new high school. Would I have had the chance to tell them I was just months away from walking at the first graduation that my school had ever held—as a member of the top 5 percent of students, at that? Would they have cared that I was an amateur writer and a track-and-field captain just getting some exercise in my off-season?

You see, prejudice, if we break it down etymologically, basically means to "pre-judge." This can be useful in dangerous situations. It's what allows us to read a scene and pick out someone or something that is out of place. But when this function is racialized with negative stereotypes, we get inaccurate and often harmful readings. This is why police officers can be more suspicious of Blacks and Latinos. This is why after 9/11, most of America gained widespread distrust of Arabic people and Muslims—many of whom were just as shocked and heartbroken by the tragedy as the "average" American.

Now, you may have heard the phrase *systemic racism* and wondered if it's real. Remember that racism implies an imposed imbalance of power or opportunity based on racial identity. The word "systemic" refers to racism that's been integrated into our social institutions. While a lot of work has been done to counteract it, you can find its residue in institutions such as our education sector, our housing and real estate sector, our credit and financial sector, and our business sector.

To illustrate what I mean, I want to share a little bit about my own educational journey. From kindergarten to second grade, I went to an elementary school just a few blocks from my house. My great-grandma would walk me there sometimes, and sometimes my mom would set me up on the handlebars of her bike and ride me over. I don't remember much from that school except for a girl with blond hair who I had a small crush on and a couple of older students who always seemed scary. (You know how, when you're little, the big kids just seem to tower over you like giants?)

I also remember being bored all of the time and my mom grilling me about not doing my homework. In my young mind, though, it didn't make sense to do a whole math sheet if I understood the lesson after two problems. I got good test scores, but I wasn't challenged. What I didn't know was that my teachers were thinking of putting me in remedial classes even though I tested higher than my classmates.

My mom moved me to another school the next year. It was on the other side of town in a predominately white community where, as she told me later, standards were higher, and teachers cared about their students. It turned out to be true because that school had technology I'd never seen at my first school. The teachers there also talked to me and asked me about my interests. One even realized that, though I was a slow reader on oral exams, my comprehension was second to none. She gave me more challenging books for reading assignments and encouraged what would become a fascination with reading, whereas I had hated reading before because I was made to feel like I was bad at it.

So, what could cause such a gap in the school experience? It clearly has to do with money and not race, right? Well, yeah. Schools with more funding can hire better teachers and afford better resources. The question you have to ask, though, is where is that money coming from? Many cities fund schools with money from property taxes. Nicer communities with more expensive houses generate more property taxes. Unfortunately, due to a practice called *redlining*, African Americans have historically been blocked from living in some of these communities.

In the decades after the Civil War, government officials would take maps and draw red boxes around parts of the city that were considered undesirable for investment and development. Can you guess who lived in these areas? To complicate matters further, bankers and investors used these maps to deny people access to loans (and later credit), which meant they could not move into better areas. This created a disparity between the communities and the resources available to them that haven't been entirely corrected, despite efforts. These are some of the things we're talking about when we discuss "white privilege," which we'll explore more in-depth in the next chapter.

Another term that you may have heard is *reverse racism*. This usually comes up in conversation when a white person feels like they've been discriminated against because of their skin color, usually by members of a minority group. As an example, I want you to consider the discussion around white people wearing their hair in dreadlocks. If you do a quick Google search on "Should white people wear dreads?", you'll find a slew of links pointing to all of the reasons why they should or should not be *allowed* to do what they want with their hair. Black opposition often cites it as cultural appropriation (the adoption of an element from one ethnic group's culture by another group without homage to the original culture), while white supporters claim that denying them that personal liberty is reverse racism.

I recently had a conversation with a good friend about how his younger cousin was told that she should cut her dreadlocks because it is a "Black thing" and she is not Black. Rightfully, they were both very upset because their Scottish ancestors actually wore dreadlocks. They hailed from a lineage that wore the hairstyle, and being told they weren't allowed to because they were white was both offensive and inaccurate. Now, my friend is *not* insensitive to the landscape here in America. He's the furthest thing from prejudiced that you can get. So, when he asked me for my take on white people with dreads, I knew it was simply to try and understand why Black people were so angry. (I'm so lucky to have him as a friend!)

What I told him was that I don't personally care what people do with their hair. Personal liberties should be protected for everyone, of every skin color. I did not, however, consider the sentiment that white people shouldn't wear dreadlocks to be reverse racism. The reason is quite simple if you remember our working definition of racism from earlier. Because people of color do not have the *power* to enforce discriminatory practices against white people, it is not a form of racism. On the other hand, on American soil, ethnic hairstyles such as dreadlocks, afros, braids, and cornrows have been relegated to black people almost exclusively. In particular, dreadlocks and afros have been called "distracting," "dirty," "unprofessional," and "inappropriate" and used as a discriminatory reason to force Black people to conform to white standards. I remember a news story about a Black high school student being told to cut his dreads so he could walk at graduation. I also remember the countless hours my sister spent on her hair so it would never look "ghetto" or "unkept" in public. (Do you see the imbalance of power at work?)

Whenever you hear the term reverse racism, remember that it is a misnomer. What that person is really referring to is racial prejudice which is the problem that this book solves. You'll learn later how you can confront prejudice in yourself and others.

I hope that by reading this chapter, you are starting to get a peek into ways prejudice and racism have seeped into the modern world. The key takeaway here is that you've been taught racism looks like lynching and segregation when in today's reality, it should include such issues as economic disparities, judicial inequalities, and even bias against Black expression by way of hair and clothing styles. Like I said in chapter 4, this is not stuff that has just occurred, but rather is just a part of the ongoing narrative. There has been progress over the years to create more "equal" opportunities, but we have more work to do in building true equity in our society, and that, I believe, starts with creating more empathetic people who can see the problems that still exist.

~

Definitions We'll Use Going Forward

- **Race**—generally based on the expression of phenotype, race is an *artificial* social structure that refers to groups of people who share significant biological traits such as stature, facial features, skin color, and hair texture.
- **Prejudice**—preconceived, and often irrational or unjustifiable, negative emotions or evaluations directed at people from other social groups.
- **Discrimination**—the unequal treatment of a person or group based on their status (age, religion, ethnicity, sex), often by limiting access to social resources.
- **Racism**—prejudice and discrimination against individuals or groups based on beliefs about one's own racial superiority, resulting in unequal distribution of power, resources, and social status between racial groups.

Reflections

What are some basic stereotypes you have accepted about different social groups? Have you ever made a snap judgment about a stranger based on one of these preconceived notions? In what ways did or didn't the person live up to your expectations?

Chapter 6

Talking about Privilege

"All animals are equal, but some animals are more equal than others."
— George Orwell (*Animal Farm*)

Growing up, you were probably taught that all men and women are created equal, that everyone should have the same opportunities in life and nobody should get any special treatment. You may have been taught that in America, you get what you work for, no more, no less. If you treat people fairly, work hard, and never give up, you're sure to be successful. Now as an adult, you've maintained that belief and would consider yourself moderately successful because of it.

Chances are, the idea of "white privilege" just simply didn't make sense in this world because you've always worked hard for what you wanted. Someone calling you privileged simply for being white probably sounded rude and prejudiced, right? That's a totally understandable response. How can you be privileged if you have to work for a living?

This was the case for Ashley, a woman I had gotten into a debate with online. I was scrolling through my newsfeed when I saw her post to a page I follow. It read, "I'll not apologize for being white or be told my skin color makes me somehow privileged. Anyone who tries to make someone feel bad because of their skin is a racist." Clearly, she had some strong feelings about this, and I assumed someone had called her privileged more than once in her life. Looking at her profile, she looked like the average white Gen Z American. If her photos were anything to go by, she grew up middle class, probably went to a nice school, maybe had a few well-off Black and Asian friends, and no one probably talked about race except to joke about stereotypes. (Of course, this is all conjecture!) [1]

For some reason I still can't explain, I felt compelled to comment. So, I wrote, "Interesting take on racism."

To my surprise, she responded with, "I just don't believe in white privilege."

Where would this conversation go if I kept talking? "Okay cool. Why not?"

"My family isn't rich, and we won't be getting extra help for my college tuition. My parents both worked to pay for their college. How is that privilege?"

"Makes sense. Those are good questions. I see how from where you're standing there is no privilege in that. You're looking at wealthy people getting into college on money and connections. You see *some* minorities getting a little extra aid to make sure they get in. You're too normal to get shit. Does that sound right?"

"Yeah pretty much."

"See, I get you. LOL. For discussion's sake, could you accept you got it better than a few people?"

"Sure, but it's not because of race."

She was friendlier than I thought she'd be. She must have thought the same thing, since she was still responding. I replied, "Are you sure? Do you live in a relatively safe neighborhood? Do most of your neighbors look like you? Does your community recognize you as valid without a descriptor? Have you ever been afraid that your encounter with an officer might be your last if you don't 'act right and comply with every order?' Have you ever been followed in a store just because you don't look like you belong?"

"No, but what's that got to do with it? Like, I see what you're trying to say, but that doesn't look like privilege. It's just life."

"Exactly! That's normal life for the average American. Would you believe me if I told you that's not normal for some people? Would you believe me if I told you that while there are poor people in every "race," poverty looks different if you're a minority?"

"Maybe. The media is always talking about how poor Black people and Mexican people need help. They forget about us."

Ah, now we were getting somewhere. "Got it. Sounds like you don't feel seen. Keep going. Please, say more words."

"Wow. uhm. ok. LOL. Yeah, the media makes it look like white people don't need help. Like we don't work for anything because we're white. Some of us do need help and I shouldn't have to feel bad or guilty about needing help. You know? Why is it just because I'm white, I have to feel bad that I don't have it as bad as the other guy when I don't feel that way? I'm not a bad person."

Ashley had an excellent point. She wasn't a bad person at all, if our short conversation was any indication. What I told her is what I want you to consider now. Not being privileged in some ways doesn't mean you aren't privileged in others. The truth is, you are better off than some folks. It's okay to say it. You'll always be better off than some people and worse off than others. (It doesn't mean that you're a better or worse human being.)

What's not okay is that some of the ways in which you may benefit, others won't have the opportunity to reach—or they'll have hurdles to jump that you don't have to face. Their racial identity means they'll face challenges that don't exist in your world. If you can see how you're better off than some groups in ways that they can't possibly overcome on their own, you can make a difference. This is where *equity* comes in.

Equality, as described above, is a great ideal to strive for, but not necessarily what we need right now in order to close the gap. It means treating everyone the same and giving everyone access to the same opportunities but ignores that some people are starting a few steps behind due to racist practices that we're still dismantling. Equity, on the other hand, ensures everyone has what they need in order to benefit from those opportunities. This means that anyone starting the race from behind the starting line is given a short head start or ends their race an equal number of steps early so that everyone runs the same time or distance.

Equity acknowledges that while an African American, a Latino, and a white student might all come from low-income households, it's for entirely different reasons. One hundred and fifty years of segregation and discrimination barred many who were descended from slave status from attending universities, receiving loans, owning property, or having significant business presence, making it more challenging for Black families to accumulate inter-generational wealth and valuable job skills. Second- and third-generation Latino immigrants may lack the financial history in their families to get standard financial aid—especially if their parents were undocumented. Poverty in a white household may be due to a family business going under, and rising educational qualifications forcing formerly middle-class earners to take low-paying jobs or accumulate massive debt in order to stay competitive on the job market.

Sure, all three families may have to work hard for what they have presently, but skin color and ethnic background played a role in creating obstacles that were largely insurmountable for people of color, resulting in the wealth and educational disparities we see today. So, while equality means everyone today will be treated the same, equity recognizes each of those three might need different levels of help in order for them to have equal access and opportunity for the same level of success. Put another way, equality allows us all to run in the same race, and equity ensures that we all have the same starting conditions. It acknowledges that while some groups would receive more aid, they had a restriction imposed on them that made the gap larger in the first place. It's about counteracting privilege created by a white supremacist system.

Sure, it's not "fair" that Ashley won't get extra government help getting into college. But no one will assume she's uneducated or be surprised if she gets a degree at all. She'll never have to work twice as hard to gain the respect of people who see her skin color and assume she needs pity or she's some anomaly success story. Her future children won't wear a label that marks them as a secondary group in society. She'll never be forced to choose between her natural hair and having a professional job. She has all of these forms of personal privilege because society legitimizes her normalcy. Still, none of this makes her (or you) a bad person, and no one wants you to feel like that.

Your personal privilege is not the problem. The problem is the biased system that creates the privilege. That is a system that keeps people of color from advancing their place in society at faster rates. If you want to help (and I assume you do because you're still here), you have to understand the ways you benefit from the system because those are the ways in which minorities have been held back. It may be as inconsequential as seeing faces that look like you in movies and television or as significant as seeing faces like yours in public office. Or it could be that you feel safer with a police cruiser parked on your street while your Black friend is deciding if he might need to leave or if it'd be safer for him to wait (even though he's done nothing wrong).

If there is anything you take away from this chapter, it should be that acknowledging that white privilege exists and working hard to understand how it benefits you personally is not the same as confessing your sins in church. It is choosing to see that the equality we were taught we have will take a little more striving to reach. The only thing stopping us from doing that (which can be taken as good or bad) is our willingness to admit that there is a problem. Think of it this way: If you got sick, you wouldn't pretend you were okay and hope it went away. You'd start taking medicine and eating soup and drinking more tea and orange juice. You treat the problem as best you can. Right? Shouldn't we take the same approach with problems in our society?

So, if you've done all the reading to this point, this is the time for you to get excited. Your efforts are about to be rewarded! Up until now, everything you've learned has been about seeing and understanding the problem from a historical context. While there is so much more to learn, you should now have a sufficient level of knowledge to begin the work.

REFLECTIONS

Think back to my conversation with Ashley and apply the questions I asked her to your own life. Do you live in a relatively safe neighborhood? Do most of your neighbors look like you? Does your community recognize you as valid without a descriptor? Have you ever been afraid that your encounter with an officer might be your last if you don't 'act right and comply with every order?' Have you ever been followed in a store just because you don't look like you belong? Do you believe your answers are indicative of some level of privilege? Why or Why not?

CHAPTER 7

GETTING TO THE CORE OF THE PROBLEM

"Until you make the unconscious conscious, it will direct your life and you'll call it fate."
— Carl Jung

When I decided that I was going to write this book, I set to work with two fundamental questions in mind: "Why is racism so hard to get rid of if we all know it's bad?" and "Will changing laws and policies be enough to get rid of it?" To start exploring these questions, I want to tell you about a conversation I had with my friend Ebony.

A few nights before I started writing, Ebony and I were chatting about an interesting post she had shared on her social media feed. It read, "Anti-racism work is NOT a self-improvement space for white people. If protecting Black bodies & empowering Black lives aren't at the center of your work, then you're not here for Black people— you're simply going through the motions to make your white self feel better."

At the time, it struck me as a little counterintuitive. Didn't we *want* white people to work on themselves? Wasn't self-improvement one of the goals? I sent her a text message, and we hopped on a video call to talk about the "role" of white people in supporting Black Lives Matter and our quest to end racism for good.

"I'm all for people making positive changes," she said, "but don't co-opt our movement and use it as an excuse to hype yourself up and talk about the 'work'"—she made air quotes with her fingers —"you're doing. They need to learn real Black history, not just slavery. They need to show up to protests and vote for more minority representation. You know?"

"Well..." I said. She had a good point. "I think you're right. There is more urgency for people to be active like that. But I think the self-improvement is important too because a lot of people still don't understand why we're pushing for social change. You know? The whole reason we still have this problem is because white people haven't been working on themselves to drop the racist thinking and prejudice programming. If they fix their thinking, their actions would change."

That last line is the defining point of this story. What I wanted Ebony, and now you, to consider is that racism, like many of the world's problems, has deep roots in the psyche. The societal problems are symptoms, but the real sickness is inherently mental.

In order to understand racism in the world as a mindset problem, I want to point you to two of the core principles I learned while studying Hermetic Alchemy. Hermes Trismegistus is considered the father of Western alchemy, and without getting too far into his lore, I'll tell you that what he taught had less to do with changing lead into gold and more with transforming one's mind (a precursor to psychology).

The first principle is "The Law of Mentalism," which states, "All is mind." The second is "The Law of Correspondence," which says, "As within, so without."[1] To put it simply, these two concepts posit that everything we see in the world can be considered a manifestation of our own minds. That is, everything that we create as a society has to become real in the mind before it becomes real in the world—including racism. This is important to understand because it offers a clue to answering my two questions. It's also the basis of the work you'll be doing in the next half of this book.

You see, if everything that we create is a manifestation of what's inside of us (or our social consciousness), then the existence of racism in the world is evidence of its existence within our minds. It is both a social *and* a personal problem, and it persists in society because it has not been addressed within the people who make up society. Furthermore, if we *only* deal with racism in our institutions and continue to ignore our own personal prejudices and misconceptions (which are racism's driving forces), we'll not be able to get rid of it once and for all. The inverse is also true, though: if we change what's inside, we can change what we create.

Now, I know what you're thinking. You're *not* prejudiced. You have non-white friends. You don't judge people or treat them differently based on their family or skin color, and you've never agreed with discrimination. You think white supremacy is a disgusting idea. Well, what if I told you that you actually *do* have prejudice and *do* support and benefit from white supremacy, and you simply can't see it?

In chapter 5, we discussed how prejudice can show up in small ways, such as harmless stereotypes. Now I'd like to revisit prejudice from a slightly different angle called *unconscious bias*. This term refers to social stereotypes and beliefs about people you form outside of—or below the threshold of—your own awareness. It's often tied to subliminal associations you make based on things you see or hear; however, as the term implies, you don't even know you're making them.

Normally, when someone makes you aware of a bias, it's pretty easy to spot—like having a left-wing or right-wing political stance—and you can start consciously counteracting it. However, sometimes you make associations that are harder to see and understand because they are too deep in your subconscious. Psychologist Sigmund Freud taught that the mind is like an iceberg: one-third is above the water (your conscious mind), and the other two-thirds is below the water (your subconscious mind). According to Freud, the subconscious mind is the primary source of human behavior, and this is where unconscious associations and biases are created.[2]

His student, famed psychologist Carl G. Jung, took this concept further with his theory of the *shadow self*.[3] You can understand the shadow self as a collection of the repressed aspects of your identity. These are aspects that you find so shameful or unacceptable that you couldn't possibly imagine yourself having them. So, your mind pretends they don't exist by hiding them deep in the subconscious.

If this is taken as true, then it poses two significant problems: (1) these aspects don't go away, but instead manifest in unexpected, often irrational behaviors; (2) it blocks you from exploring any biases or behaviors attached to an aspect hidden within your shadow. This is generally what happens when it comes to talking about racism. Because you're taught from a young age that racism, discrimination, and prejudice are all bad, you internalize the idea that these are the worst sorts of people, creating a negative connotation around anything associated with them. So, even if you are then taught prejudiced thoughts or behaviors from your parents or develop them from things you see in the media, if you're not simultaneously taught that they are prejudiced, you may not see them as wrong.

This creates a huge internal rift between how you how act and how you perceive your actions. Because you've internalized that racism is bad, if someone says you've done something racially offensive, you also might react with anger as if *you've* been insulted. This is your shadow acting out to protect you from feeling guilt or shame from personally identifying as a "horrible" racist person. This is the reason why so many white people are triggered by the idea of white privilege. In their conscious mind, they're thinking, "How dare you say I'm a bad person! I believe everyone should be equal." Meanwhile, their subconscious mind is running racist programs (such as assuming that a person of color stopped by the police *must* have been committing a crime, even if absent of clear evidence).

What all of this means for you is that in order to start dismantling your unconscious biases, you'll have to learn how to recognize and confront your shadow. You have to become aware of the unconscious programs running in the background of your psyche and affecting your judgments and behaviors. Once you can look into your own darkness without feeling triggered, then you can effectively identify and counteract the little biases and stereotypes you hold. You can have conversations with people and engage with broader history without feeling personally attacked. This integration of the subconscious and conscious minds is a process called *shadow integration*.

When most people hear the terms "shadow integration" or "shadow work," their minds usually conjure images of witches or voodoo queens calling on shadow-y figures for strange occult rituals. If this is the image you've got, you can rest assured that this is *not* the work we'll be doing in this book. Contrary to popular belief, in most cases, the term "shadow work" refers to the process of exploring the unconscious mind and becoming familiar with the mental processes that affect our everyday lives.

For the purposes of this book, I'm going to treat bias and prejudice like a bad habit. I've found that the steps for overcoming a bad habit are also ideal for exploring the subconscious mind. To illustrate this point, I want to tell you about a time when I had to dive into my subconscious to get rid of a bad habit.

Believe it or not, there was a time in my life when I had a seriously bad "relationship" with sugar—and when I say bad, I mean it's almost embarrassing to talk about. I kept an ungodly collection of sweet snacks in my filing cabinet at my old job (Mystery Oreos, chocolate candy, pie, etc.). It wasn't until my body gave me a subtle clue in the form of recurring chest pains and trouble breathing that I realized I actually wasn't super healthy anymore, and it just might be time to cut back.

It wasn't easy. In fact, more often than not, it proved impossible to turn down "just one cookie" or "only a scoop of ice cream," even though I knew I didn't need it. Any time I got a good streak going, I wound up having to start over. This went on for weeks until I had an epiphany while telling a friend about why I hated pulling weeds.

"Many of them are designed to break off at the stem," I told her, "leaving the roots intact underground. To pull the whole weed, you have to loosen the roots."

It dawned on me then that I was going about things all wrong. The real reason that I couldn't just drop my sugar habit was because I was pulling that weed from the stem and not the root. On the surface, it looked like the weed was gone, but it always grew back before too long. In this analogy, you can think of the active habit as the body of the weed—the part you see above ground. There is still a whole root system below ground that you can't see; that is the source. I wasn't able to crack my habit because I had to learn how habits are formed.

I'll spare you any more confusing psychology. All you need to know right now is that the mechanism behind the formation of habits is subconscious association, or relationship. If the mind experiences a repeated association enough times, it generates a subconscious pattern. (If you're curious about this, you can read up on Pavlov's dog experiments.)

In terms of racial prejudice, you can consider negative media representations of people of color as an example of associations impressed on us—you know, Arabic people as terrorists, Blacks as gangbangers, and Mexicans as unintelligent or as criminals. The subconscious pattern that forms is a mistrust of these racial groups. This may manifest as calling the police for "suspicious activity" when you see an unfamiliar face in your neighborhood, overlooking certain job applications, avoiding working with specific clients or partners in your business, or keeping a close eye on possessions when your kids bring friends over. And you may not even realize you're doing these things.

Going back to my (not so) sweet situation, I spent some time thinking about why I really kept so much sugar around. More importantly, what was the benefit or satisfaction I got every time I ate sweets? Obviously, I loved sweets because they made me feel good. From here, I did a thought experiment and asked, "If it's true that I eat sweets to feel good, could it also be true that without them, I did not feel good?" Going along with the experiment, I said yes (which was true anyway since I was under constant stress from work). This implied that I had made an association between sweets and relief from stress.

Now I had the key. It turns out, if I accepted this as true, I could trace this pattern back to a time in college when cookies and ice cream were my go-to's to deal with stress during finals week. (Didn't seem so bad at the time!) Five years later, though, I had slowly built an emotionally and psychologically dependent relationship with sugar that was directing my behaviors against my conscious will. Suffice it to say, sugar is not a problem for me today. Through the steps that I'm going to reveal to you shortly, I was able to dive deep into my shadow and unpack all of the unconscious thought patterns that kept me attached to a negative behavior.

Now, I know your problem is not "How do I stop eating sweets before I develop a series illness?" Yours is "How do I eliminate racism and prejudice?" Even so, the work to solve them is the same. You'll have to dive into your shadow like I did and start unpacking all the hidden mental programs running without your awareness.

There is a good chance you've never heard about any of this stuff, and that's okay. You wouldn't unless you study psychology at the university level or, like me, you have a thirst for personal development. But aside from being a little esoteric, there is another reason more people don't know about, let alone implement, this type of work. Can you guess? *It's hard!* Carl Jung himself admits it, saying, "The shadow is a moral problem that challenges the whole ego-personality, for no one can become conscious of the shadow without considerable moral effort. To become conscious of it involves recognizing the dark aspects of the personality as present and real. This act is the essential condition for any kind of self-knowledge."

Even so, the steps of shadow integration are more intuitive than you'd think. The steps below are explicitly tailored to tackle subconscious bias. Let's take a look:

Step 1 – Define Your "Why"

The first step to integrating the shadow is pretty simple. "Defining your 'why'" means recognizing why you want to begin this undertaking and see it through. A clear motivator gives you two essential keys to success: (1) a goal or value that can compete with your innate desire for comfort, and (2) a reason to commit to this decision. What's more, clarifying a goal makes it more real. Without a goal, it's hard to visualize what success looks like, and as we know, to manifest anything (including change), it has to become real in the mind first.

Step 2 – Acknowledge Your Shadow

Because the shadow represents the aspects of ourselves that we have subconsciously rejected, it's common for people to deny that it exists. Since you've committed to doing this work, you must remain open to the idea that you can and will find out things about yourself, many of which will be unsettling. Get as comfortable as you can with two major ideas: (1) some of the qualities that you hate the most, that you find the most embarrassing, deplorable, and triggering actually exist within you, and (2) by repressing this side of yourself, you've cut yourself off from seeing when it misbehaves or how it influences your decisions.

Step 3 – Analyze Your Behaviors and Interactions

Earlier in this book, you saw examples of how racism shows up in innocuous ways, often in what we say and how we act and *react* to people of other races. Take some time to look seriously at your behaviors. Do they look or sound like anything you've read in this book? For instance, have you ever felt inexplicably tense or on alert while around people from other races? Once you have a few scenarios, do some thought experiments like I did. Take it as true that some of these behaviors have racist origins and then try to find the root. What feeling led to that behavior? What thought led to the feeling? Where did that thought come from?

Step 4 – Rethink Your Thoughts

As you follow the cognitive behavioral chain above from action to emotion to thought, you may start to find an inherent logic. Everything has an origin deeper in the psyche. So, what comes before thought? *Perceptions.* The things we take for granted as facts (with and without evidence) generate thoughts—snap judgments—which lead to our eventual behavior. These perceptions and assumed facts are where unconscious biases and stereotypes hang out, informing your judgments and manipulating your behavior without conscious behavior. By following this chain and exposing the biases, *you* hold, you identify the misconceptions and traces of prejudice in yourself that you are operating under and passing on.

These are the thoughts that allow you to unsee white privilege. You may find a thought that says, "White people are more trust-worthy than Mexicans." Consciously, you may not have that bias, but a part of you must, otherwise, you wouldn't tense up around Mexican people you encounter. Otherwise, you would feel just as comfortable hiring and doing business with them. You see what I mean? Your actions and feelings are evidence of the thoughts and biases that exist.

Step 5 – Practice Mindfulness

Now, the moment you identify a thought that you don't like (such as "whites are more trustworthy than Mexicans" or "Black men are more aggressive/unpredictable/dangerous than white men"), your immediate reaction might be to try to eliminate it right away. Your ego will think, "Oh, no! Where did these awful thoughts come from? These aren't me. We have to change them right away and never have them again!" You must resist this urge, and here's why.

There's a saying among manifestors and mystics that goes, "What we resist persists." This means that if you actively reject these biases as detrimental and evil, they won't go away. Conversely, if you accept them as a part of yourself, they go away. In a more occult world, the explanation is that when you accept that you have these thoughts, the part of you that has them becomes fulfilled, and the energy is free to move to a different thing. For practical purposes, I'll say that by learning to accept that you have negative biases, you give yourself ownership over them. This is different from embodying them, wherein you choose to continue the behaviors that come with them.

If you own them, you can be aware and counteract them when you notice they are coming up. Before, you didn't know it was there. When a thought like, "These Black men are dangerous and will rob me if I'm not careful" came up and evoked a fear emotion in you, you went with it, likely without even noticing. Now you can recognize when you're feeling fear, trace it back to the thought, and ask yourself, "Is it true?" The only true thing happening in this example is that the men are Black, and you don't know them.

Step 6 – Forgive Yourself

Along the same lines as the previous step, you need to forgive yourself for having bias and prejudice. You see, they are there for a reason—and not just that they were passed down systemically. Each one persists because it is serving you in some way. I know what you're thinking. How can these be good if I'm supposed to be getting rid of them? That is a *perfect* question, and I invite you to consider this: what if your preconception that Black men are dangerous was triggered as a way to keep you safe? What if you're not from a diverse community and everything you've seen about African Americans shows them as aggressive? Could it be that the association between Black men and danger was created in your young psyche as a way to protect you from becoming a victim?

Understanding the function it's serving allows you to understand *why* it is there without feeling guilty and wanting to run from it.

While ultimately you do want to counteract the bias, an important step in releasing it is releasing your attachment to it. You do this by acknowledging how it serves you, appreciating its service, and then committing to replacing the biases with thoughts that are more aligned with who you are and the person you want to be. For example, "Black men are dangerous" is a subconscious bias that can be easily transmuted into, "There are Black men here." Then, with time, that too could become something like, "Black men are here minding their own business and I'm in no immediate danger." The next thought from there is, "Men are here minding their own business."

Step 7 – Decide New Behavior in Advance

Finally, you want to decide in advance how you'll respond to both your triggers and the stimulus. When you plan your response before a trigger happens, you give yourself an exit strategy from your default behavior until your new behavior becomes your default. It takes the pressure off of you to decide in the moment and removes the chance to have that internal dialogue. For me, it was to verbally affirm to myself that my goal to cut sugar had more value than the cookies and Snickers bars, and then to do something to keep working. For you, it might be to mentally remind yourself that stereotypes in the media are biased input, and you're not going to believe them in real-life interactions.

∼

As I close this chapter, I just want to acknowledge that this has been another intense chapter. You've covered a lot of ground! The content you've just read is not your everyday discourse. It was written specifically for you because you are brave enough to take on the murky waters of the mind and find what lurks within. It is the more challenging path, and I can't stress enough how proud I am that you have committed to this process. You've certainly earned a small reality break before diving into the next chapters, where we explore the work involved in counteracting racial prejudice in society.

REFLECTIONS

How do you feel in spaces filled predominately with people who do not look, think, or talk like you? Does your body react? What emotion is attached to that reaction? Can you identify a belief attached to that emotion? Where did that belief come from?

CHAPTER 8

THE ILLUSION OF SEPARATION

"The greatest illusion in this world is the illusion of separation."
— Albert Einstein

I n all the previous chapters, we've discussed what racism is, how it looks, and how to find it within yourself. In this chapter, I want to get to the heart of the matter. (Yes, we can go yet one more level down the rabbit hole.) You see, even indoctrinated bias and prejudice have roots in something far more inconspicuous—though arguably much more dangerous to a unified society. It's a mental process called *otherization*[1] that allows us to recognize ourselves as distinct from anybody else.

On the surface, this is harmless. You are you, and I am me. Neither of us is our parents, nor are we identical to anyone else. Makes perfect sense, so what's the problem? Well, imagine you've got two kids, twin boys. When they were first born, they might have seemed inseparable. It must have been so cute watching them sleep all tangled up together. As they got a little older, they probably shared almost everything too, from cuddles and kisses to food and toys. And whenever one would cry, the other would start too. That's because, at this early stage of life, they're still new to the idea of a unique self. To this point, they were essentially almost one because they both shared that same sacred womb space within their mother.

Now they're a little older—let's say two years old—and you're noticing different behavior. It's subtle at first, but you can tell they aren't sharing as much. When one reaches for a toy that the other has, the second instinctively pulls away. One day, they're playing, and one boy wants a toy so badly that he pushes his brother and takes it. As you're trying to console the crying toddler, you find yourself scolding the other one for his aggressive behavior. "Why did you do that?" you ask, as if at two years old, he would be able to answer you.

Anyone who has kids knows that these types of squabbles don't end at age two. In fact, you might find yourself asking each kid that same question a hundred times without getting a straight answer. So, I'm going to give it to you now. It's because each child has developed a unique self-identity, an awareness of himself as separate from his brother, which allows him to take action against the other without feeling it as affecting him.

From this metaphor, you can see the ability to do harm to someone is directly related to your ability to detach from that person. It's not too far of a stretch, then, to imagine that one social group's ability to wage war and subjugate another group is directly related to their ability to see the other group as separate. This is that feeling of "not one of us" at play. The inverse of this is that in order to cause harm to another person or persons, we have to first see them as separate from ourselves. And, in fact, this is precisely what happened when the African slave trade came under fire back in the late 1700s.

To put it briefly, when European imperialists were in the middle of their conquest of Africa, many countries were ending the institution of slavery (viewing it as against the teachings of Christianity). So, slave owners and traders had to find a way to justify enslaving black Africans—who, by the way, had once been at the top of the social hierarchy. (You can look up Mansa Musa and his empire or Egypt prior to Arabic conquest or even Moorish rule in Spain to learn more about African prominence in history.)[2]

In order to protect the slave trade, its supporters assembled a wide arsenal of claims and "scientific" theories about Black people, which they then codified and spread in all manner of literature, from books to cartoons. Many of these claims were that Africans were innately inferior, barely human, uncivilized, and savage. Africa was slandered as being so barbaric and chaotic that its inhabitants were far better as slaves. You can find plenty of examples of this in an eighteenth-century book called *History of Jamaica* by Edward Long[3], a British slave owner who lived in the British Caribbean colonies his whole life. It was this sort of deliberate dehumanization that allowed for racism to move beyond a capitalist tool and into the social consciousness.

So, if otherization is so dangerous, why do we do it? And how do we stop doing it? Well, it's not inherently dangerous because it is completely natural. If we didn't have this mental process, we wouldn't understand things like boundaries or the unique "I" or other personal pronouns. So, there's no way or reason to actually *stop* it altogether. What you can do, though, is learn to see through it to the truth that it's only a trick of the mind, a function of consciousness.

The Einstein quote I opened this chapter with is often used to refer to his discoveries in quantum physics—namely things like quantum entanglement, which asserts that everything is affected by (and thus connected to) everything else. In spiritual teachings, this same quote is used to summarize the theory that we are actually all one consciousness having individual experiences that contribute to the whole. No matter how you align, it's clear that we are all more connected than we recognize.

To overcome the illusion of separation, we must learn to see each other in ourselves, or at least ourselves in each other. We can do this by applying what you've learned so far to cultivate empathy. In the next chapter, you'll see how empathy actually helps us get around otherization so we can start building a world with less prejudice.

REFLECTIONS

What is one social group or demographic that feels utterly foreign to you? This is a group that may feel like your complete opposite. Think about the *humans* in this group. Are there any similarities? List as many as you can, and then note whether your feelings about them change a little.

CHAPTER 9

THE MAGIC OF EMPATHY

"Thou shalt love the Lord thy God with all thy heart, and with all thy soul, and with all thy mind. This is the first and great commandment. And the second is like unto it, Thou shalt love thy neighbor as thyself. On these two commandments hang all the law and the prophets."
— Jesus Christ (Matt. 22:37-40 *KJV*)

Ruminating over the words above, I want to draw your attention to the second great commandment: "Thou shalt love thy neighbor as thyself." This is actually my favorite scripture in the entire Bible because it encapsulates the essence and the aim of empathy, which is to reciprocate love to others as if to yourself. Without getting into a discussion of Biblical epistemology, I want to share what this excerpt reveals to me about how we should live and how we can use this for the purpose of confronting prejudice.

You see, it's actually closely related to the golden rule, "Do unto others as you would have done unto you." When I think about how I want to be treated, words like "respect," "dignity," "compassion," "kindness," "consideration," and "valuable" come to mind. Likewise, I've *never* wanted to feel left out, unimportant, like I was unworthy, like I was a bad person, or like my feelings didn't matter.

What these two famous quotes ask me to do is consider whether I make other people feel any of these things (either good or bad). Do my words and actions put people down or build them up?

Love is a force that makes things better—more beautiful, more radiant, more joyful, more kind. Love gives the recipient more potential to grow and thrive. Love forges bonds that give people and objects purpose. It's a value-adding force that brings out the recipient's best qualities. As a short thought experiment, I invite you to think back to how your mother or grandmother treated you as a child.

When you were hungry, did she give you food? When you were cold, was a blanket draped over your shoulders? When you were sick, was she there to check on you every hour? When you were afraid of the dark like I was, did she walk you to the bathroom in the middle of the night? When you got awards in school, did she clap and squeeze you in a big hug? When you came up with a new game to play, did she pretend to understand the rules and make sure you felt like you won?

On your birthday, did you always get a cake, card, and song no matter how old you got? At Christmas, did you always have presents under the tree no matter how many times you thought you made the naughty list? At Halloween, did she tailor your store-bought costume to fit you just right for trick-or-treating—and still remember to bring your jacket for when it got cold?

Now that you're all teary-eyed (because I refuse to admit I'm the only one who gets choked up thinking about my mom and my grandma), I want to make just one thing clear: *that* is love. The feeling beating in your chest now is how it feels to know that you are genuinely loved by somebody, and you know that because of the way somebody treated you. So when Jesus says, "Love thy neighbor as thyself," I take that to mean remember this feeling and make sure everything you do reflects and creates this for others. When you love someone, you desire for them to be as blissful as you are.

Seeing someone suffering and feeling bad for them is sympathy. Seeing someone suffering and recognizing that they, like you, had a mother who loved them—that, like you, they have hopes and dreams and fears—and using that understanding as a way of relating to them, that's empathy. Empathy is looking at another person and seeing that they are just like you and choosing kindness instead of adding to their burden.

The skills you learned in the previous chapters were all about understanding yourself better. I want you to consider now that everything you found within yourself—the good, the bad, the beautiful, the ugly, the inspiring, and the painful—is also in every other person. You've met yourself so intimately and learned how to treat yourself with compassion. If you can see your neighbor as someone with the same dreams and struggles as you, you can use what you now know about yourself to be a little more sensitive to their experience, since they're like you at their core. This is what it looks like to get around "the other."

One tool that helped me tremendously when it came to understanding people at a fundamental level was Maslow's Hierarchy of (Human) Needs. All you need to understand here is that Maslow theorized that all humans have the same fundamental needs, without which they could not be truly fulfilled in life. He broke them into three primary categories, each with sub-categories, as follows (starting from the base of the pyramid and ascending):

Basic Needs (most fundamental)

- Physiological needs—food, water, warmth, rest
- Safety needs—security, safety, shelter

Psychological Needs (most communal)

- Belongingness and love needs—intimate relationships, friends, community
- Esteem needs—prestige and a feeling of accomplishment

Self-Fulfillment Needs (most abstract/cerebral)

- Self-actualization—achieving one's full potential, including creative activities

I was amazed when I first read this because it not only made perfect sense, but I could also see myself in it very clearly. I *do* need food, water, and shelter. I recognize the desire for community and for intimate relationships. What's more, I know how it feels to chase this hazy idea of a fulfilled life. This opened so many doors to understanding people. When you understand Maslow's hierarchy, you begin to look at people and start asking important questions.

For example, what is your first impression when you see a homeless person holding a cardboard sign at a freeway exit? Personally, I always wrestled with whether giving them money was considered charity or enabling. After seeing Maslow's hierarchy, I realized that that man on the corner just needs to eat. If I were in his worn-out shoes, I would pray that someone—any one of the hundreds of drivers using that ramp to get to homes and jobs I may never have—would notice me and maybe spare enough change so I could get a couple of fifty-cent tacos and maybe some sunscreen or bug spray. It's hard to judge a man who lives like that.

What this looks like in terms of our conversation about racism is looking at Black teenagers walking down the street and remembering that they want to go home like everybody else does. It's seeing your Latina coworker and remembering that she wants to feel valued and to know that her ideas matter. It's walking past a birthday party at the park and considering that maybe the Pakistani family is just trying to enjoy their day with close relatives. In seeing the basic humanity in the people around you, you allow yourself to relate to them, which allows empathy to grow some roots.

The funny thing about empathy is that, like love, it cannot be taught within the pages of a book. I can teach you *about* it and leave you breadcrumbs so that you'll know it when you see it. However, understanding empathy at a mental level will not be enough to teach it nor to use it to drive prejudice out of people. The only way to do that is to model it, to exemplify it. We have to assume that people who don't practice empathy don't know what it looks or feels like, so telling someone about it is like trying to capture all of your mother's love in two paragraphs. You too will have to show empathy in order for people to learn from you.

Even so, I know the effects of empathy are so transcendent and powerful that I've actually done my best to model it to you in the pages of this book. Think back to chapter 1. How did you feel after reading it? If you're this far in, I can only assume that it's because you felt safe—that is, like I understood you. You probably felt like you could read this book without being judged. Then you made it to chapter 3, and you knew without a doubt that I understood exactly where you were coming from, why you were here, and how you were feeling.

By showing you that I understand—that I care enough to acknowledge you and see your struggles without judgment—I was actually using empathy. I put myself in your shoes as best as I could and asked, "How do I feel right now? How do I want to feel?" and the answer came back: "I feel nervous and unsure if I'm doing the right thing. I want to feel seen and heard and like I can actually do something helpful." I was able to use the very strategy I'm teaching in order to win your trust, at least enough to keep you turning pages.

This is how you, too, will get others to understand your message. By leaving an example for them to follow, they will always remember how you made them feel. When your words and actions make people feel safe and heard, they are more inclined to keep listening. This is why Jesus drew the crowds he did. I don't necessarily consider myself a person of "the faith," but I know that the archetype of Jesus was so attractive because, unlike other images of God throughout history, he showed up with a message of compassion. He forgave people, told them to be better, and put his faith in them to rise to the bar he set for them. If you take the Bible to be true, then he set the precedent for how each of us should love.

All that being said, empathy is a very simple thing, and chances are that you practice it regularly without realizing it. I know I have many times with coworkers. There is one incident when I was working my department manager job that I don't think I'll ever truly forget.

During the weeks leading up to Thanksgiving, stores would get slammed with turkeys and other frozen goods to ensure good stock for the holiday. Because this would be nearly twice the regular freezer capacity, the company would send a refrigerated trailer for the overflow, and somehow, no matter where I worked in the store, I always seemed to end up outside in that trailer.

On this day, there were five of us (all Black) out there sorting and stacking turkeys, pies, and frozen vegetables by date and rotating product inside to the main freezer. It was cold and unforgiving work, only made worse by the fact that it was snowing in Colorado Springs already.

As I stacked what felt like my hundredth turkey, my coworker said, "Did you notice how all the Black people in the store today are out here in the cold? How did this happen? None of us even work this department."

"Don't even get me started," said another coworker. He was young like me.

I had noticed, but being the only supervisor in the crew, I didn't want to be seen instigating anything. I said, "Yeah. But it happens we're also all in departments that aren't really priorities today."

"Nah," said the first coworker, while he wrote the dates on a stack of frozen carrots, "I think Roland's racist."

Roland was the manager on duty that day. He was an older white man with white hair slicked back like Elvis Presley and an unmistakably Texan accent. He gave off this sort of shady salesman vibe, like he spent his younger days talking people into buying cars at the sticker price and calling it a deal. I never really pegged him for a racist, though. Not until he came out to check our progress.

"Boy, y'all are out here working hard," Roland said. "You're doing real good, ya know. Now, I don't know if any of you have ever had the pleasure of picking cotton."

He paused.

We paused.

Time paused.

Did he really just say that? I thought. We stood there staring, him at us and us at him, stalemated like a lion and a pack of hyenas.

He continued, "Because I have, and let me tell ya, it's a tough job. I just wanted to say I appreciate the work y'all are doing." With that, Roland went back into the building and the five of us were left there dumbfounded.

I wouldn't have believed it if I hadn't lived it. What did he mean, "the pleasure of picking cotton?" My coworkers all wanted to quit right then—and they would have been right to. But I couldn't afford to, and this work needed to get done. So I swallowed my feelings and persuaded them to help me finish the load, and if they felt like leaving for the day after that, I would vouch for them.

They stayed, we finished the load, and I contemplated reporting Roland. I thought about his comment for two days until the store manager was in. I was prepared to tell him everything. On my way to the manager's office, though, I ran into Janice, who told me she was just talking to Roland, who she claimed had been crying. The store manager had just chewed him out pretty badly over the condition of the store and some other employee complaints.

"He's scared he might get fired soon." She said.

There it was. Something I could relate to. That fear of losing a stable income and sense of security. That feeling of being two inches tall in front of the store manager. (If there was one thing that man was exceptionally adept at, it was dishing out tongue lashings.) I knew exactly how Roland felt, and, despite my feelings about his comments, I couldn't bring myself to say anything that would make his difficult situation worse. Sure said something ignorant, but I didn't want to take away everything. Maybe there would be a better time to talk about it. For the time being, I decided to return to my job on the sales floor.

For the first time, the veil of separation had been pulled back to reveal something undeniably human about Roland that was easy to miss when I was focused on how offended I was. I allowed him to be a person like me, and that allowed me to have compassion. Today, I tell people this story to demonstrate how sometimes our choices can affect others. Can you think of a time when you saw how your actions could have negatively impacted someone? Did you go through with it or choose a different path? I invite you to think about the outcome and how you can use that testimony to guide your choices and teach others about compassion and consequences.

Overcoming prejudice and confronting racism today hinges on our ability to embody empathy. In order to teach people to be better, we'll have to *show* them the way. I don't know if Roland was actually racist or if he was sincere in his compliment and looking for a (misguided) way to connect to us. But I know that he, like most people, had room to learn. When we act with compassion, which is the active form of empathy, we close the gap between ourselves and other people. We heal old wounds and open the door for people to have different dialogues. Empathy allows us to meet people where they are instead of toiling to bring them to our level, and that is the only way I know of getting people to show us their hearts so they *can* be swayed.

REFLECTIONS

Think about a time when you felt judged and wished someone had understood your situation and shown you compassion. What was happening? How did it or how would it have felt to have a little bit of grace at that moment? How can you do that for others?

CHAPTER 10

COURAGEOUS CONVERSATIONS

"Human conversation is the most ancient and easiest way to cultivate the conditions for change—personal change, community and organizational change, planetary change. If we can sit together and talk about what's important to us, we begin to come alive. We share what we see, what we feel, and we listen to what others see and feel."
— Margaret Wheatley

One night, a couple of years and a promotion after the incident with Roland, I was working the closing shift as a salaried manager when I got a call on my walkie from one of my frontend supervisors, "Assistant manager Andrae, can I meet you somewhere?"

"Is it urgent?" I asked. "I'm touring right now and will be passing that way in a little bit."

"Yeah. I can meet you where you are," she said.

"Okay. Garden Center."

When she arrived, she had this mischievous grin on her face. She was distressed but looked like she might break out laughing.

"What's up?" I asked.

"So, I didn't want to say anything but I don't really feel comfortable working in the cash office with Dennis."

"Did he say something?"

Her cheeks turned red and she covered her mouth with her hands, perhaps to hide her smile. "No. He stinks. Really badly. The whole office smells like him, and it's making me nauseous."

"Oh, geez. Okay. I'm on it. You run the floor while I figure something out." She nodded and went back to the registers. *Just great...* I thought. Why did it have to be on my shift? Why did I always get the awkward situations? As a manager, it was a part of my job to talk to associates about hygiene, but really, who wanted to be the person who tells another grown person they stink and need to put on some deodorant or something? It was going to be another one of those uncomfortable conversations that came with the badge...

When it comes to ending racism, you're going to be positioned to have your fair share of uncomfortable conversations. Now, I don't really like that word, "uncomfortable." Something about it just screams, "Brace yourself because you're not going to like what comes next." You know? While I was training to be a manager, we used a different word: "courageous." The thought was that if we go into it with the mindset (and language) that this was going to hurt, we couldn't do anything about it. By renaming it a "courageous conversation," we were telling ourselves we had the courage to take action and the power to lead effectively.

In my role, there was no turning away from things that made me uncomfortable. I was specifically there for others to turn to, which meant I was the last line of defense. The buck had to stop with me. Whether it was dealing with an upset customer who hated the service they got, giving an honest eval with an underperforming associate, or (in this case) an associate whose odor made it difficult to be near him, my job was to make sure that the correct information was delivered in the best way possible for that specific situation.

In the same way, doing this work will put you into positions where, in order to make a difference, you cannot turn away. You'll have to discuss things like white privilege and white fragility with relatives. You'll have to talk to your colleagues about discrimination in the workplace. You'll have to your kids about prejudice and what to do when they see injustice. You'll very likely be in direct opposition people who think the only reason racism is a problem is because Black people—and now people like you—keep talking about it.

To continue on this path, you're going to have to draw from your well of courage in order to meet the darkness in yourself and others time and again and bring it to light. Your knowledge positions you as a leader in the conversations that society is having, which hang almost entirely on our ability to communicate effectively. Since it's such a critical skill, I wanted to take a second to share with you a few invaluable tips I've picked up from my time as a manager. While these conversations are more complex and intimidating than talking with an employee about hygiene, this conversation illustrates some essential elements to navigating these discussions confidently.

No. 1 – Prepare

Whenever you sense you have a conversation coming up—or a situation where the potential for a courageous conversation is high—you can save yourself a lot of trouble by getting prepared. This can mean having your facts together or having a space ready. It can also mean thinking about who the other person in the conversation is and how they tend to react or building up the mental fortitude you'll need in order to move through the conversation without getting triggered yourself.

I was the one who had hired Dennis and given him a chance despite his failing the interview. He and I also had a pretty good rapport because I spent as much time as I could training him so that he felt supported and encouraged in his role. Because of this, I knew he'd be very amicable when talking with me. Even so, it's a sensitive topic, as some people have medical conditions that make them sweat more. The last thing I wanted to do was make him feel bad about something outside of his control. The right words and location would need to be chosen ahead of time.

I wanted him to be aware of the problem and open to discussing solutions with me. Saying something insensitive would destroy the trust he had in me. There was also the chance that calling him to the manager's office would set the wrong tone, so I planned to approach him in the cash office. This meant, though, that he could feel cornered.

When you're about to have a courageous conversation, be mindful of what your ultimate goal is and all the factors that could affect it. (Remember Who, What, When, Where, How, and Why.)

No. 2 – Read the Situation

In normal life, it's not often that you can prepare for a courageous conversation ahead of time. They're more likely to spring up in the middle of a nice dinner or during a lighthearted chat at the office. And even if you manage to prepare ahead of time, things inevitably come up that you couldn't have planned for.

When I approached Dennis in the cash office, the first thing he said was, "Did Megan send you?"

I sighed and answered, "Yeah... so then you know what I'm here for, huh?"

"Yeah, and I'm sorry. I have a lot going on right now and the embarrassment is making me nervous. I can't stop sweating."

Before I had said anything, Dennis knew what was on my mind and had started telling me what was going on. This gave me two crucial bits of information: (1) he trusted me, and (2) he felt really guilty and embarrassed by the situation. I also guessed that Megan had said something to him before coming to me. With that information, it was evident that I could skip the script and talk to him a little more personally. More importantly, it was obvious that he was ready to talk and my first responsibility was to listen.

When you have tough situations come up unexpectedly, you're going to get an initial fear response. You're going to tense up and wonder what to do. Read the situation. Look for clues in the person's tone and body language and let that inform how you can react. Consider things like how they're acting if other people are around. For instance, could they be putting up a front for others? If so, they may be more prone to lash out if you make them feel embarrassed.

No. 3 – Listen Actively

"Well," I said, "would you like to tell me a little about what's going on? I totally get that it's personal, but there may be a way that I can help you."

"Thanks, Andrae," he said, "I don't know if you or the store can help, but basically, my apartment building doesn't have any water right now, so I haven't been able to wash clothes. Normally, I wash a load every couple of days because of my condition, but I've had to re-wear clothes in between trips to my mom's."

How awful. I couldn't believe one of my associates was going through something like that. "I see. That's terrible. I'm sorry that's happened to you. Do you need a fresh uniform to get you through the next couple of days? If you stay under a certain dollar amount, I might be able to explain the expense."

"No, no, it's fine. I'm going to my mom's tomorrow and I'm going to stay there until the water is fixed. And on my lunch, I was going to buy some more deodorant and body spray for my locker."

Dennis was in a really tough spot, but it turns out he was already working on his own solution. He was embarrassed but doing the best he could with what he had. I couldn't help but be proud of him.

What I want you to take away from this, though, is that he did *not* need to be told the policy. He didn't need to be told he had B. O. or to wash up or get extra deodorant. He needed me to listen. And by tuning my ear to what he was actually saying, I learned vital information about him *and* continued to foster the good relationship we had.

If you're having a courageous conversation with a relative or someone you consider a friend and want to preserve the relationship, the worst thing you can do is focus strictly on what you want to say while bypassing what's actually coming up in the conversation. The biggest reason conversations turn into arguments is that one or more parties feels like they can't get their point across because the other is not listening. We all want to be heard, so if you're going to lead the conversation, be prepared to listen.

No. 4 – Speak Clearly

Even though Dennis had explained his situation, I still had a problem to solve, which was that work needed to get done but his peer couldn't work with him. It was up to me to make a decision and communicate a plan of action. Of course, that would mean also explaining the situation from my perspective and what would happen if we didn't resolve this.

"Wow," I said, "I'm glad you have somewhere to go in the meantime. And I love that you've thought through a solution. So, here's where we're at. Megan doesn't feel comfortable working in this office with you because of all of this, so we have to do something. If it's alright, I'd like only one of you to be designated for cash office tonight."

"Okay."

"I'd like for you to be that person. With your current condition, it might be easier on you to have less face-to-face time with customers, and we run a lower chance of offending any of them. You won't have to stay in the office, but Megan will run the floor, and you'll do cash office. We can revisit this after your lunch. Does that work for you?"

He went along with it happily. What is important here is that even though I completely understood Dennis's situation, I still had to be honest and clear about exactly what I was saying. My understanding allowed me to do so more lovingly. As you navigate your own courageous conversations, remember that having empathy and understanding does not mean you shouldn't say what is important.

Rather, it gives you insight into how and when to say it. But it's still up to you to be clear.

For example, if you're having a conversation about white privilege and financial aid, it may come up that whomever you're speaking with is not privileged because they had hardship but they got no extra help. Since you know that white privilege exists, you can and should still speak to that. You may just want to make sure that you say it in a way that easily distinguishes white privilege as benefitting from the advantages white people have had in America as opposed to framing it as white people having everything handed to them.

No. 5 – Anticipate Resistance

In this conversation, Dennis was pretty amicable. You cannot expect every conversation to go this way. What would have happened if he didn't like the solution I proposed and said something more like, "I think making me stay in the cash office is unfair. Why should Megan be the only one on the floor? I've been helping customers all night and haven't offended anyone. I think you're singling me out and taking her side."?

This is one of those unexpected occurrences that can come up. It would be all too easy to flash my manager badge and say that I've made up my mind—or to get upset myself due to time being wasted on a busy night. We only had a few hours before closing anyway, so why would it be such a big deal?

If in this hypothetical, I responded like that, it would have been a disaster. I would say something along the lines of, "Okay, I can see how you'd get to that conclusion: you staying back here and doing all the cash office work while she gets to interact with people and move around. It looks like I'm giving her what she wants." In this scenario, instead of trying to prove why my decision was better, it would have been more beneficial to slow down and show Dennis that I understood and that I was listening because that trust was lost. I would have followed that up by asking "What would you like to do?" This would have made way for him to articulate what his needs were.

In terms of race conversations, some people will be resistant to the idea of having privilege, like Ashley was in chapter 6, or to the notion that saying, "All Lives Matter" makes them racist. If you are committed to seeing the conversation through, it can be helpful to have them state their case as clearly as possible and explain their position to you. Then repeat back what they said in your own words. You might say something like, "So, if I heard you right, 'Black Lives Matter' is racist because it only promotes Black people and nobody else. Can you tell me more about what exactly you think Black Lives Matter means? It sounds like you're saying it means Black people are more important than everyone, and I want to make sure I understand you here."

I use this approach all of the time because it allows the other person to continue to have a voice while simultaneously feeding me all the information I need to understand the root of their problem —the false thought that is triggering all of the misconceptions that usually come up. Some people jump at this opportunity. Others will feel like you just don't get it and try to shut down the conversation by deflecting. Understand that this is because you're getting closer to the truth and making them do a lot of heavy lifting and unpacking. Most people don't do this consciously, but it is a form of resistance that you'll encounter, and helping them to get around it will require that you are adept at managing your own emotions using the insights you've learned in this book.

When it comes to dismantling racism, people will tell you it's about swift, decisive action—supporting equality efforts and pushing for better legislation. I hope that through the course of this book, I've shown you that while those things are essential to addressing the immediate symptoms of racism, in order to eliminate it for good we have to cure the disease itself, which is the hidden bias and inherited norms built into American culture. This is something that is challenging us to up-level our ability to relate, which means also up-leveling our communication.

I've just given you five tips to do just that. Of course, there are many other things you could consider, like delivery and resistance, but by mastering the skills presented above, you'll be well-equipped to find your way through most of the conversations you'll need to have. As a rising leader in social change, you have the message that people need and the heart to deliver it. I encourage you to take these cues and use them to lead your own courageous conversations—your movements—with tact, grace, and ease.

REFLECTIONS

Having courageous conversations can be hard. In what ways could you create or foster *brave* spaces to have open and honest conversations about prejudice, discrimination, and racial equity? Who do you know that is modeling the courage you wish to have?

CHAPTER 11

TAKING DIRECT ACTION

"Every great dream begins with a dreamer. Always remember, you have within you the strength, the patience, and the passion to reach for the stars to change the world."
— Harriet Tubman

Growing up, I absolutely loved superheroes. There was something about the larger-than-life portrayal of brave people putting on colorful costumes and saving the day that captivated me. Maybe it was the way "good" always won in the end. Or the way Superman, Batman, or Spider-Man (my Big 3) could swoop in and do the things that the police officers couldn't. Superman was my favorite, of course. He could do everything, he was never late, and everyone loved him.

I remember watching *Superman: The Animated Series* and feeling a wave of pride swelling in my chest every time his iconic score would start to play. It didn't matter how bad things got in Metropolis, the moment I heard it—low fanfare rising steadily; a loud *whoosh* accompanied by a red-blue-blur streaking across the screen; someone shouting, "Look! Up in the Sky!"—I knew *it was on!* I cheered right along with the cartoon officers and citizens as

Supes arrived just in the nick of time. We could all breathe a sigh of relief.

I still love Superman today, although my reasons are less to do with how he can smash through walls and fly and shoot lasers from his eyes (come on, *that* is cool), and more to do with what makes the Man of Steel so inspiring to me: his ideals. We all know he's famous for upholding "truth, justice, and the American way," but he also believes in compassion and kindness. He believes in helping people whenever and wherever he can. It doesn't matter who you are or how you look, he believes in the potential of every person to be a force for good in their own way and that by doing good, he can inspire others to do so too.

I don't know if you're a Superman fan—maybe you're more like Han Solo, a smuggler looking out for his friends—but the fact that you've made it this far is proof that you do care about doing the right thing, even if it's not always clear exactly what that is. In this chapter, I want to highlight a few ways that you can start making a difference right now. Some of them may seem small, but remember, even little things matter, and to quote Mother Theresa, "We can [all] do small things with great love."

Continue Learning

As I talked about in chapter 4, racism is nothing new to this country and the conversations that we are having now have *all* been had before. One of the most valuable things you can do is start to learn more about the other (non-white) side of history in America. Read some books and watch some documentaries. This is important to deconstructing false and incomplete narratives that allow for things like white privilege to exist unchallenged.

For instance, have you ever put much thought into the Civil War and what really sparked it? While the issues of taxation and state's rights to autonomous governance are touted as large factors, if you read South Carolina's and Mississippi's declarations of secession, you'll see that the country's growing polarization on the issue of slavery is pointed out more than once. This history may seem insignificant now, in 2020, but these are the things that created a bitterness toward Blacks in the form of Jim Crow, which we discussed previously.

Believe me, I'm the last person you'd probably see willingly pick up a history book. I totally get any resistance you're feeling. But what I had to learn is that when you study history, you can make the connections that allow you to see current events *in context*. The more you know about what happened and how it evolved into what's happening, the more you can actually see. What you're able to see in the world is determined by how much you know about it. The less you know, the easier it is to miss things because your brain doesn't have a word or concept for the thing you're looking at. For instance, you and a carpenter might look at the same cabinets and see totally different things because his knowledge of craft makes him more aware.

Now, I do want to offer you this caveat. As you start to explore alternative accounts of history, it may feel like the voices sharing them have an anti-America or anti-white-people sentiment because the facts do not always present white Americans very favorably. I would encourage you to lean in anyway and have your own experience with the facts so that when you're confronted with opinions and information, you can always speak intelligently and confidently. Remember the mantra I gave you at the end of chapter 3. It's not about learning to be angry at our shared history, but about balancing your knowledge and using it to stop recreating the past. You can never overcome something at the same level of awareness that created it. You have to stretch your mind.

That being said, here are the names of a few notable authors and scholars whose works should help you to get a more total-box view of our history in this country:

- Frederick Douglas
- Dr. Sebi (Alfredo Darrington Brown)
- Malcolm X
- Ta-Nehisi Coates
- Angela Davis
- Maya Angelou (If you prefer fiction and poetry)

Also, here are a few notable resources that you can read right after this one:

- "White Privilege: Unpacking the Invisible Knapsack," an article by Peggy McIntosh
- *Waking Up White: And Finding Myself in the Story of Race* by Debby Irving
- *How I Shed My Skin: Unlearning the Racist Lessons of a Southern Childhood* by Jim Grimsley
- *White Like Me: Reflections on Race from a Privileged Son* by Tim Wise

Talk to Your Children

Now, I know the last thing anyone wants to do is tear the magic out of a kid's eyes by bashing them with harsh truths—so don't do that! But it's incredibly important for our children to hear from you, their parents, what's going on in the world. Children today have access to more knowledge than any generation before them, and it's instant. The trouble is, not all of that information is factual or useful. As our society continues to develop, we have to be aware that there will always be those who resist progress and continue to spread detrimental viewpoints. It's up to us to make sure our children have a way of interpreting what they see and hear.

When I was a kid, I was perfectly content with Saturday morning cartoons and sugary cereal. All I had to worry about was getting my homework done and staying out of trouble. Would you believe me if I told you my sister and I had to talk to our younger sister (age eleven) about suicide after she heard her friend was thinking about self-harm? I didn't even know that was a thing until I got to high school and sat through uncomfortable videos in health class that did nothing to help my understanding of depression other than scare me into thinking it would lead to death.

I say all that to illustrate that our children need us to engage with them. How can we protect them if we don't know what they know? How can we fight prejudice if we don't talk about it with them? I remember a time when my oldest sister and I were walking in Redlands and a group of white teens drove past us in an uncovered Jeep shouting, "Niggers! You bunch of niggers!" I'm sure some of them just thought it was the cool, fun thing to do, but I have to wonder what made them think shouting racial slurs at people was cool or fun in this decade.

Diversify Your Business Network

Think about all of the places you shop and all of the people you've hired. Were any of the stores "Black-owned?" Were any of the realtors, lawyers, mechanics, or technicians you hired from a "minority" group? I'm not saying there's a problem if the answer is "no." People generally tend to shop in their own communities and in places that they trust. If you want to support the advancement of people of color, consider shopping around. There are many industries where you can find hardworking, reliable entrepreneurs from a variety of backgrounds.

If you're a business owner yourself, you can internalize this in your company by diversifying your hiring. Believe it or not, studies are finding that applicants with "white"-sounding names are twice as likely to get a callback than those with "ethnic" names. Let's say you're the franchise owner of a local restaurant chain and you're looking for a manager. If you get applications from Shelley O'Hare, La'Juana Jackson, and Francisco Ramirez and all three have equal qualifications, will they all get an interview?

If you want to promote diversity and inclusion in your professional space, the most impactful thing you should do is double-check your own subconscious decision-making. Does any part of you *feel* like Francisco would be a better fit before you even met him? Why? Perhaps because he is a man? Does Shelley make you think of your aunt who was always hardworking? Does La'Juana's name conjure doubts about her education or work ethic? These questions represent the snap judgments we all make unconsciously, and they are all based on prejudices and stereotypes that we've taken for granted. You have to be aware of the unconscious biases informing your business decisions in order to consciously counteract them.

To promote diversity and inclusion, you would make sure each candidate not only gets an interview but is given fair consideration. It may also require recognizing the needs of your community. If the site that needs a manager gets a lot of Spanish-speaking customers, having someone who speaks Spanish can go a long way toward making them feel welcomed. If the site is in a predominately Black community with many Black applicants and patrons, your business can support this community by having jobs available for them.

Additionally, you may want to consider widening your talent pool. When you sit down to review applications, you should consider how diverse it is from the start. If your restaurants are located in multi-ethnic centers but your applications don't reflect the same diversity, you might delay hiring until you've tried other ways of finding talent. For instance, if all of your applications come from an online portable, you can post a "Now Hiring!" sign at the door to make sure people who frequent your business know to ask about applying.

Now, if any of this is starting to sound a little like giving people of color preferential treatment, let me assure you that it's not. As a former retail manager, I totally understand the stresses of finding and hiring strong candidates. When it comes to choosing who's got the best chances of success, it can sometimes come down to small details like how well-prepared someone is when they show up for the interview or the charisma they show when answering your questions. It often has nothing to do with race, and I would never encourage giving preference to anyone based on racial background —in fact, doing so is both in violation of EEOC regulations and the antithesis of this book! What I am encouraging is finding ways to make sure your hiring reflects the needs of your business and the demographics of your community by actively looking for candidates who may be qualified but under-represented.

Support Equity Efforts

In chapter 6, we discussed privilege and the difference between equity and equality. As you start to take corrective action against racism in society, you can research initiatives geared at promoting equity in your area and show your support by voting and signing petitions. Stay current on bills and propositions. Pay attention to local government officials and candidates running for office. Hold them accountable to their promises and the voice of the community by calling or writing letters to local government. Give support to candidates who keep their word or elect new officials when they don't.

Another important factor in creating equity is supporting minority representation in public office. Often, municipal leadership can be misrepresentative of the region's true demographics, and you can support their inclusion by supporting their causes or the representatives who do. If you become aware of injustices or imbalances of power in your community that can be corrected, imagine if you were in that group, learn about what's going on, and lend your voice. If you're able to, donate to causes geared at driving change and bringing about more equity until everyone has an equal shot at the American dream.

These are just a few ideas about how you can get started, trusting that you'll use what you've learned so far to find ways that work with your situation. If you can't support financially, you can show up to protests. If you can't protest because you're deathly allergic to tear gas, you can vote. If you can't register to vote, you can raise awareness within your network and commit to personal change. The point is to align your actions with your beliefs (which is the secret to all conscious manifestation).

So, just to recap, I suggested four ways you can support social change, which are to continue learning, talk to your children, diversify your business network, and support equity efforts. You don't have to give up your whole life in the name of social justice activism (unless that's always been your life dream), but if you do even a few of these things, you'll be well-positioned to be a part of the solution.

REFLECTIONS

Great change is created by the sum of small ones. What are some easy commitments you can make today to take just one step toward being the change you wish to see? What do you think would be the impact of these changes in your personal life and communities?

CHAPTER 12

NOT AN EASY ROAD

"Success is not final, failure is not fatal, it is the courage to continue that counts."
— Winston Churchill

Unlearning generations of white privilege and subconscious racial bias is not going to be easy or immediate. It's immensely personal, difficult, and existential work that may make you feel things you don't fully understand. You might become embarrassed. You might feel anger toward other white people who aren't putting themselves through the same intense work. You might even question more than just your thoughts about race.

You see, shadow work challenges you to question everything you previously took as secure, and exposing unconscious racial bias may make you question if you really are a good person like you thought. (How could you be if you never saw these things, right?)

But because of this intense work, committing to this process will do more for you as a person than eliminate racism. It will radically transform your way of thinking by opening your mind to things you couldn't see before. It's the work that will allow you to "check your privilege" and walk a mile in the other guy's shoes. It'll empower you to take control over your thoughts and notice when you're not living in alignment with what you actually believe. And most importantly, it will allow you to model better behaviors to future generations and help your children to navigate the tough discussions they will undoubtedly have as they grow up and continue to spread change.

In this chapter, I wanted to take a minute to point out some of the challenges you'll run into while implementing these steps in hopes that when they do arise, you'll be prepared to deal with them.

No. 1 – Doubting What You Find

As you go through this journey, you'll be confronted with information and ideas that are in direct conflict with the worldview you've been raised with. Very quickly, you'll start to see some of the things that you learned about history (for example) are actually incomplete or told from just one side. The skeptic in you won't want to believe everything you find. Naturally, you may find yourself trying to cross-reference and fact check as much as you can to make sure it's actually true—and that's a good thing!

Do you remember when Wikipedia got really popular and people were using it to read up on almost everything? Well, after some time, it became clear that the popular information hub was not a reliable source of information because anybody could create a page for a topic and even edit existing pages, and there was no one in place to filter credible facts from opinion and false information. This is exactly how the internet is now. You'll find information on almost anything, but there is no guarantee that it'll be true or useful.

Just remember to keep an open mind. Where too many go wrong in their research is that they gravitate toward resources that validate their previous worldview. It is imperative that when you find these books, articles, and videos, you consider if they present the whole picture. Did the creator do research? Did they address counterarguments to their claims? Did they reference anything that you can look up for yourself? My advice is to take *everything* with a grain of salt and cross-reference as much as you can. The point of research is *not* to find objective truth (although I know you'll find some) but to see the big picture, that there is more to the story than the conventional narrative reveals.

No. 2 – Resistance

Previously, we talked about facing resistance from others during courageous conversations. What stops people from succeeding with these steps, though, is not resistance from others but from themselves. When confronted with questions that challenge your integrity, your first reaction is to reject them. It is a natural self-preservation tactic that the ego employs because it is built on all the beliefs you've accumulated to this point. What this leads to is an innate resistance to the discoveries.

You're probably going to feel like I'm full of crap. You're going to want to say this shadow work, psycho-analytic stuff is not for you. You might even put this book down thinking, "Well, that's not what I was looking for" or "That was interesting, but I'm not a racist, so I don't need these steps."

These feelings and all the others that come up for you are entirely valid and natural. You should listen to them. Then use this process on them! Really, you can totally do that. The steps you learned about uncovering the origin of thoughts and the thought-emotion-feedback loop can be applied to these thoughts as well. For example, if you think, "I'm not a racist, so this book doesn't help me," I'd invite you to ask yourself how you're feeling when you decide to put the book down. I bet it has something to do with fear, stemming from misconceptions that the work is too hard and the misguided thought that you can't do it and you're going to fail. These ideas stem from the subconscious preconception that if you learn something bad about yourself, you're a bad person. So, instead of opening yourself to feeling vulnerable, your shadow conceived a way to invalidate the work.

Don't fall into this trap. The steps work if you can be gentle with yourself. It is hard, which is why 90 percent of people in the world *don't* engage in this level of self-work. You can be in the other 10 percent. In fact, you must be if you're going to help lead the world through empathy. It starts with practicing empathy toward yourself. This brings me to the next major pitfall.

No. 3 – Not Enough Patience

Because this is such intense work, it's going to take time to implement and get used to practicing. The "purification of the soul" is a life-long process of refinement. There is no point at which you're "done." You just get progressively better as you continue the work.

Where so many people lose traction is that they feel like it's taking too long. I remember when I helped my friend get over a bad breakup. Her ex had been cheating on her and she didn't find out until he finally left for the other woman. She was so torn at first, but over time she started to heal. One day, she asked me about my last breakup and if I still thought about my ex.

"Yeah, sometimes," I said.

"Oh, really? Does it still make you upset?"

"Not really. I mean, I'm not particularly happy when the thoughts come up, but they don't bother me."

"How long did it take you to get here? I feel like no matter how hard I try, I can't stop having angry thoughts about him."

He had broken up with her five months prior and she was way better off than when it was fresh. What she didn't understand was why negative thoughts still came up sometimes. What I told her is almost exactly what I want to tell you: even after all of this, you probably will still have thoughts that are rooted in racial prejudice. They are a part of your upbringing. The result of the work is not that you'll never have another racist thought, but that you'll be able to recognize when they come up and let them go as quickly as possible because you know that they're not true. Over time the thoughts will change, but you have to be patient with yourself and trust the process.

No. 4 – Feeling Disconnected

This is a big one. The irony in doing this work to bring more unity and equality is that (at least initially) it may leave you feeling a little disconnected from people who aren't on the path that you've chosen. The curse of knowledge is that, to an ignorant person, you sound completely crazy. As such, if you have relatives or friends who don't want to join you in diving into the black lagoon (the shadow) you'll reach a level of understanding that will set you apart from them.

That's not to say that you'll be better than them. No, it's more like trying to talk about foreign countries to someone who's only read about them from the comfort of home. They won't see what you see right away, which can make communicating and relating a little challenging. It's like the Millennial generation explaining to their Baby Boomer grandparents why nobody spanks children anymore.

This feeling of isolation can be enough to make anyone want to stop digging. But I encourage you to keep going. Remember that the point of this work is not to make anybody change or see things your way, but rather to learn how to relate to others. By doing this work, you'll understand yourself so much more intimately, and consequently, you'll be able to understand others more deeply than they understand themselves. This will allow you to have more compassion toward them, and compassion brings people together.

No. 5 – Trying to Change Everyone

Okay, this is *the* big one. Have you ever been in an argument with someone that just didn't go anywhere? Did it feel like the other person just wasn't understanding you, no matter what you said or how you said it? How did that argument end? My guess is with two angry people with hurt feelings, maybe a lot of distance for a while too. Right?

The thing about arguments is that each side is usually too busy trying to prove the other person wrong to hear what the other person is actually saying. With everything you've learned in this book, I'm sure when the time comes that you find yourself "debating" white supremacy with someone, you'll try listening and understanding to see if you can get inside their heads and reason with them. I, having taught you this method, have to warn you that there will be times that it flat out doesn't work. (Wait, what??)

That's right, in some conversations, empathy and compassion won't make anyone listen to, hear, or understand you any better. The reason for this is that people can only meet you as deeply as they've met themselves. Further, people who feel so passionately that they are being attacked aren't always open to having their minds stretched. In these moments, it'll be clear that the other person simply isn't ready for the conversation. So, what do you do?

As I explained before, you have to read the situation and the energy. Listen closely for clues about where the other person is mentally and how open they are to new ideas. That will tell you right away whether it's worth the energy to engage. If you determine that it's not, my advice is to use what you know about them to practice compassion by simply listening if it's a friend, or respectfully diverting the conversation if it's not (unless you truly wish to engage).

Sometimes, these conversations can't be avoided. In those situations, speak your mind. Have confidence in what you know and the courage to say it tactfully. You're not responsible for maintaining a person's ego if they are clearly wrong. But remember, having confidence in what you're saying doesn't mean you have to be condescending in any way. For example, instead of saying something like "Well if you knew the true history of America, you'd see it's actually pretty racist," you could say, "Well, I know a few good books that talk about American history, and I was surprised to see how racism has impacted so much of our way of life, even now."

Do you see how the latter is less direct and triggering? How it doesn't accuse the other person? How it invites further discussion if they want it? It's not about proving a point in this case, but rather not compromising your peace of mind or creating unnecessary conflict. You can also refer to the books, opening a channel for people to educate themselves.

As you begin to apply the knowledge you've gained from this book, there are many more obstacles you'll run into; however, these are the most common ones I've seen. It's my hope that by being aware of them, you don't shy away from your calling. You only picked up this book because you're ready and able. Now is the right time—the best time—for you to do this work, and if you commit, you can do so much more for creating a better world than you ever thought you were capable of.

REFLECTIONS

There is strength in numbers. Who are the people close to you that are on a similar journey? How can you get connected to more like-minded people to support each other in your new direction?

CHAPTER 13

A BRIGHTER FUTURE

"In the face of impossible odds, people who love this country can change it."
— Barack Obama

W hen I set out to write this book, I had no idea what exactly was going to go into it. All I knew was that after the death of another unarmed Black man—a brother, like me—I actually had a lot to say. As I started to vocalize in various social media feeds, I was met with both criticism and support from people I barely knew. Through these conversations, I realized two things that would be central to creating something meaningful.

No. 1 – If We Listen, We Can All Relate

When I started having conversations online, I had every impulse to blast white people in the "All Lives Matter" camp with information that would prove irrefutably that racism exists and that they were making things worse by refusing to support social change. How could it not be obvious? If they just saw the evidence, it would either change their mind or prove that they really were just racist assholes. Interestingly, these were never the messages I actually sent.

You see, at the moment, I just needed to vent. Once I got past my own emotional outpourings, I inevitably found myself pounding the backspace button feverishly because what I really wanted was not to make these people feel small, but for them to understand me. And how could they understand me if I didn't understand them? What we needed in order to have productive conversations was to find common ground, something we could agree on.

This reminds me of a conversation I had with my friend Tim. He was my partner in our high school football team's video department, so we spent a lot of time together in senior year. I remember meeting his family officially in college while attending an ASU vs UCLA football game, and they were some of *the* nicest people. Not only did they pay for my ticket (I had paid for Tim's the year before), they paid for all the food and treated me just like family.

Well, in 2014, he texted me asking if we were going to get together for that year's game. Of course, I had to tell him that I was no longer attending ASU and had moved to Colorado.

"That's convenient since it was your turn to pay," he wrote. "My dad was just talking about going to Arizona too."

"How's he doing, btw?" I replied. "Is he still with the police department?"

"Yeah, he is. They're under a lot of pressure though with all this racism stuff."

"I bet. Does it make him nervous?"

"Nah. He just wishes bad cops would quit making the good ones look bad. You know he's not racist. This is all making it really hard to make it hard to do his job. People should judge him by his character, not just assume stuff about him that's not true."

Read his last sentence one more time. In a few words, my friend captured a feeling we can all relate to and which is at the heart of the conversation society is having right now. You see, nobody wants to be judged based on how they look. Nobody wants to be made out as the villain before anyone gets to know them. Unfortunately, this is what prejudice does. When we allow it to create discrimination along racial lines, it becomes racism—a disease that is difficult to cure because it tricks us into thinking that we're all different. If we learn to look past the surface-level differences, we'll find that we all have the same basic wishes and fears. This is how we start to humanize one another so we can truly stand together.

No. 2 – We Can All Do Something

The other thing I realized while writing online was that I actually had something to contribute. When standing at the cusp of social change, when everything you take for granted is dissolving, it can be hard to imagine that you can do anything. The fact that you can't imagine it, though, doesn't mean you don't have something to contribute. In fact, simply by choosing to do something, big or small, your potential to have an impact increases dramatically. That is the reason I committed to finishing this book.

I know how scary it feels to put yourself out there, to be seen taking a definitive stance and opening yourself up to other people's opinions. This book doesn't contain every possible thing you could or should do to combat racism, but it is *my* contribution to the solution. My hope is that in reading this book and incorporating the steps we've covered, you feel equipped to shoulder the weight of personal and societal change and inspired to follow my example and do the little things that *you* can. Sometimes, little things take *big* courage, but it's also these little things that matter most.

THE ROAD TO RECOVERY

It should be clear now that creating the change we need to see in the world means embodying the change within yourself. This is the true meaning of the saying, "Be the change you wish to see." While defeating racism for good is an ambitious goal that's going to take everyone's effort, over the course of this book, I've given you some key steps that *you* can take to get yourself started. Just to recap, here's what we covered.

In chapter 4, we discussed racism's historical roots and how they connect to us today. We also looked at why understanding history without taking on blame or guilt for it empowers you to be a force for change.

In chapter 5, we looked at more innocuous forms of prejudice, such as stereotypes, and how, if left unchecked, they can translate to more harmful and dangerous manifestations. We also examined some key concepts that come up in discussions about race.

In chapter 6, we deconstructed the concept of white privilege and examined how our racially divisive history has created the inequality that's felt today. You now should have a firm grasp on the differences between equality and equity and why the latter is essential to creating true equality.

In chapter 7, you began the deep work of recognizing and exploring your shadow for traces of bias that may be affecting your behaviors and attitudes. This is both a pivotal moment in the book and in you learned seven steps for taking responsibility for your mind and challenging racism where it originates: in the mind. To recap, the steps were to define your why, acknowledge your shadow, rethink your thoughts, practice mindfulness, forgive yourself, and decide your new behavior in advance. When you can apply these steps, you can guide others to do the same.

In chapter 8, I explained how otherization is at the root of bias and prejudice. It's the mechanism that allows us to dissociate from each other and therefore cause harm. This is essential to remember because it happens naturally. You must remain aware of when you're doing it if you're to be anti-racist.

In chapter 9, we unpacked what empathy really is. You learned that it's the most valuable tool we have to get around otherization and start rebuilding a sense of kinship and connection. It is only by understanding and practicing empathy toward yourself and others that you will be able to show be a lantern for others to follow.

In chapter 10, we looked at how I handled a courageous conversation in a work setting. Like I said before, if you're going to face racism head-on, you're going to have many uncomfortable conversations that are much more intense than the one I shared (not everyone can be an Ashley or a Dennis), and using these tips is going to help you. They were to prepare, read the situation, listen actively, speak clearly, and anticipate resistance.

In chapter 11, you learned the four ways I would recommend in order to start doing the work and creating changes in your sphere of influence. Those were to continue learning, talk to your children, diversify your business networks, and support equity efforts.

I believe that if you read this whole book and internalized its messages, you are adequately positioned to be a powerful inspiring leader in your home and in your communities. As I explained in the last chapter, it won't always be easy (if it were, we wouldn't need this book!). Even so, the value of this work will be felt in all of your interactions. That makes it worth the effort.

A BETTER WORLD

I want to leave you with just a few final thoughts as you set out to be the incredible world-changer you're meant to be. The decision to confront racism is one you should be extremely proud of. Getting started can be intimidating for a number of reasons, such as seeming like a sell-out to friends who don't understand, seeming insincere to the people you want to help, or simply not knowing which steps will make a difference. It's also, as you now know, a decision to confront the deepest parts of yourself and consider the possibility that you've contributed to something so vile.

Despite all of that, here you are. *You* decided that enough was enough. *You* decided you wanted to be a part of the solution. Because of that, *you* are prepared to be a leader in the transformation that is happening. If there is one thing that history teaches us, it's that the world is always changing, and those who learn to change with it have the power to shape it into something much more suitable for themselves and future generations. The fact that you're here assures me that you are ready for this, that you desire this new world as much as I do, as much as the new world desires to be born.

As you take your next steps toward creating a better world, my wish for you is to have the strength and courage to keep peering through the looking glass. What you see may shock you. Friends and colleagues may call you mad (as a hatter!). Keep looking. Keep pulling back the veil. As a society, we are on the verge of becoming, which naturally means that we are simultaneously in the process of dissolving—dissolving old beliefs, old thought patterns, old structures, and old ideals. In order to deconstruct these things that are holding us back, it is essential that those of us who are committed to the vision of a brighter future continue to face the darkness and turn it into light.

This is the real work, the great work that transforms lead (base, ignorant consciousness) into gold (refined, aware, empowered consciousness), and it is only through doing this work within ourselves, dipping into the shadow and bringing more light, that we can show others the way. This is how we'll learn to see each other as one family. This is how we can build the empathy we need in order to uplift our communities and fight racism at its core.

Reflections

It can be easy to think of equity work as an uphill battle or a point-less struggle. What is one thing that gives you *hope* for the future? What is one thing you might consider doing to keep the hope alive in yourself?

Appendix 1

Belief Psychology and Community Dynamics

In chapter 8, I explained that the heart of the problem is a process called otherization (a.k.a. othering), whereby we develop our sense of personal and collective identity. In a social context, it's a mechanism that allows for social framing to distinguish between who does and does not belong to a particular community.

In chapter 9, I followed this up by presenting *empathy* as the solution to otherization, referencing Maslow's Hierarchy of Human Needs to show how we are alike. For this section, I want to spend a little time discussing how our community dynamics impact not only our identities, but our beliefs.

The first thing to understand is that our minds instinctively look for and hold onto patterns. It is an unconscious evolutionary mechanism that has allowed humanity to survive. This echoes what I wrote in chapter 7 about unconscious associations.

You can also think about it neurologically. When two neurons are triggered at the same time, they create an association which allows for learning.[1] These patterns are how we make sense of the world. They are also a part of our categorization function—meaning we use patterns to distinguish groups of like things and separate unalike things.

As we saw with Pavlov's dog experiment, though, patterns also inform our expectations. When he rang the bell and presented food, the dogs began to recognize the bell as an indicator of food. When the food wasn't present, the dogs still expected it upon hearing the bell. Now, I know we're not dogs, but our brains work in the same way. We *like* patterns, and generally, once we create a pattern or association, we believe it to be true or take it for granted as such.[2]

Here is a relevant example. Most American films feature all-white or predominately white casts, especially in the fantasy and sci-fi genres. The same phenomenon occurs in written literature as well. This is because the creators of these stories tend to be white or of European descent. Additionally, much of the history taught in American schools revolves around white American figures and European history.

What this creates is a worldview where most people are white, and most fictional characters are white. In 2008, author Suzanne Collins published her novel, *The Hunger Games*. In it, she writes a cast that is assumed to be white, with exception of a few characters. One character, in particular, is described in the book as having "dark brown skin and eyes,"[3] indicating she is a person of color (at least in her appearance, if not culturally or ethnically).

When the movie was released in 2012, many fans of the book voiced their outrage at a black actress playing the character. Many of them had overlooked or otherwise forgotten this *small* detail and assumed Rue was also a white character. It's easy to see how this happened. They had an unconscious expectation for the characters to look a certain way based on a pattern their minds created. This leads us to the next thing we need to understand: *confirmation bias*.

Confirmation Bias is a psychological term for the tendency people have to look for information, evidence, or patterns that support their existing preconceptions (beliefs). Because we like patterns and recognize them easily, we recognize phenomena that align with the ones we have taken as true.

A related concept is the *Baader-Meinhof Phenomenon*.[4] Have you ever noticed something once, like a certain type of car or the name of a band or a movie flyer, and suddenly, it's everywhere?

That's basically what this is—when something you become aware of "appears" everywhere. This comes directly from the brain's recognition function. It's like your brain is saying, "Hey, look! I know that thing!" Every time the thing appears.

I know that is a lot of psychology to take in, but if you're still with me so far, here's what you should have taken away so far:

- People make associations through pattern recognition.
- People take patterns for granted.
- Patterns of associations shape beliefs.
- The mind tries to confirm what it knows.

This is the foundation for how we learn and form our beliefs. Over the next few pages, you'll see why it is important to understand.

Now I'd like to talk about community and identity. Remember from Maslow's pyramid that one of our core needs is a sense of belonging. We *need* to belong to a group because we are, by and large, social beings.

I do want to be particular about what a community is here. From a sociological perspective, it's a social group that follows a certain social structure. More specifically, a community is a group of people who share a common sense of identity and interact with one another on a sustained basis.[5]

This could be a geographical community or a digital one. In today's world, it is extremely common for people to consider themselves members of at least one online community. The phrase I want to hinge on, though, is the "shared sense of identity." In order to belong to a certain community, one generally has to feel like they relate to the other members through shared beliefs, core or "sacred" values, and social practices.

An example of a shared identity might be one's political party or their allegiance to their nation or state. Being born and raised in Southern California, I hold that as a part of my identity. Whenever I'm around other Californians, there is sometimes an unspoken sense of kinship, especially as Californians living in other states.

Another example might be a working-class Conservative American. While this is too broad to be a community, this *identity* can lead to the formation of communities across the country. People who identify this way will instinctively connect with and seek out more people who identify this way. They'll also gravitate towards information that supports their worldviews.

This can create a polarizing effect as people become more isolated by their group identities and confirmation bias. Computer scientist Jaron Lanier, author of best-selling book, *Ten Arguments for Deleting Your Social Media Accounts Right Now*[6], describes how social media has a major hand in this.

The basic breakdown is that corporations want to influence people's buying habits. Social media companies developed algorithms that hyper-personalize their user experience in order to collect data and create a model for predictability purposes. It then suggests content based on the data. Through suggestion, the Social media company can then influence a person's behavior (clicks, views, watch-times, purchases, and group memberships).

Unfortunately, this often means playing up on people's identities. College-aged liberal Americans, for instance, may see more content in support of social change movements and activism. They may see and join groups affiliated with movements they believe in and next to no content from the opposition. When opposing views are presented, it is usually in a negative light.

This is the crux. Our beliefs (which come from our associations) both shape and are reinforced by our identities. These identities are instrumental in building a sense of belonging. Once we belong to a community, we tend to embrace the ideas of the community as our identities align. Because of the confirmation bias and sense of belonging, we tend to adopt more of the beliefs of the group through peer interaction and peer pressure (both direct and indirect).

This is how many young and impressionable individuals find

their ways into cults and other extremist groups. In a 2021 episode of the Netflix series, *the Mind Explained*, called "Brainwashing," experts explain that when people lose their sense of community acceptance, they sometimes react by "doubling down" on beliefs and identities that are the antithesis of the ones that rejected them. They explore other groups of marginalized people to find a sense of belonging.

Think of the movie *Fight Club*. What appears on the surface to Brad Pitt's character as a boxing club for men to release anger and gain support proves to be more radical as the film progresses. Over time, Pitt's character slowly adopts new beliefs, contrary to the person he knew himself to be until, at last, he completely adopts a new, radical identity.

By this point, if you're not fascinated by this psychology, you must be asking why all of this is important. The answer is simple. **Our community identities influence the beliefs we hold most reliable and important.** These beliefs shape how we see and experience the world and other people.

Even as we become more aware of this function in ourselves and start to deprogram our minds, many of the people we will meet will have worldviews that oppose our own. We may be tempted to think of them as stupid and uneducated. We may find ourselves judging them or writing them off. This only fuels the flame because they expect us to be that way toward them. The more we villainize and ostracize people from other communities, the deeper we entrench ourselves in the ideas of "other"—that we are not alike.

What researchers in *The Mind Explained* discovered is that "peer influence" can have an impact on our adherence to our beliefs. Just as marginalizing someone can drive them to adopt a fringe, underdog identity, welcoming them into your community can shift their sense of belonging (and the beliefs that go with it).

As a brief example, do you remember from chapter 3 how many of my coworkers were more concerned with political agendas and calling out liberal media bias than the fact that people had actually died? That let me know unequivocally that we were not the same.

And yet, we all had things in common. We shared at least one community: our job.

Had I *only* looked at their social media posts and never known them personally, I would have been tempted to think worse of them than they deserved. They weren't racist. They actually just didn't *see* the race problem and genuinely felt it was a narrative pushed by the news and popular media outlets. This was confirmed by the media they consumed, reinforcing their distrust of the press.[7]

(This is how we can witness the same event and see two different stories.)

Because we shared a community and a sense of belonging, I saw them for the people they were instead of just a collection of opposing ideas—which is often what we reduce people to on social media. This also made it easier for many of them to converse with me.

The psychology of belief and community dynamics is far more complex than this, but I wanted to share more insight because it is central to the work we're attempting to do. Social change is all about creating a better, broader community. To do that, we have to be able to relate, which requires not only finding common ground but also recognizing the other community identities and personal histories that other people bring to us.

We are not always going to agree on important topics. As I share in the following Appendix, we often disagree based on political identity. But if we can build new identities and bring others into them, we can at least start to re-humanize each other. You can't talk someone out of their belief systems. You can't use logic or reason because they have come to their conclusions rationally within their minds as well. The only thing you can do is change their experience of people they (or you) may not interact with regularly.

Appendix 2

Social Change & Personal Development

(To listen to the audio or watch the full video presentation, please use the link or QR code at the end of this segment.)

Trayvon Martin (2012). Eric Garner and Tamir Rice (2014). Sandra Bland and Walter Scott (2015). Philando Castillo (2016). Stephen Clark (2018). Elijah McLain (2019). Ahmaud Arbery, Briana Taylor, George Floyd (2020).

These are just a few of the high-profile cases from the last decade that have sparked intense conversation around racial justice. Now, to many of us, it seems clear that some form of change needs to happen. But the process has been slow, and contentious nationwide. And the question remains, why?

My name is Andrae Smith, Jr. When I was just seventeen years old, back in 2012, I was a scholar athlete, a model student at a predominantly white high school. I had a lot of friends from various races, but at the time, I didn't think too much about race, racism, or what have you. That is until near the end of my senior year, Trayvon Martin, a boy my age, was shot and killed while walking home. That's when I realized that it could have been me.

In 2020, after George Floyd's death, I wrote and published my first book, *Facing Racism: The Guide to Overcoming Unconscious*

Bias and Hidden Prejudice to Be a Part of the Change. In it, I sought to answer two major questions:

(1) Why is it so hard to create social change when we know that a problem exists

(2) Are laws enough to make social change last?

Whether you think that social justice is an important topic right now, or part of a political agenda, I want to remind you that someone you know, in love is or could be a member of a marginalized community. And understanding the mechanisms of social change is important, vital leaving to protecting them, and their rights and freedoms.

I've come to understand that lasting social change—big, intentional change—only happens when enough people want it to. So the key to bringing this massive lasting change to our society is to change the individuals who make up our society. Over the next few minutes, what I hope to do is show you exactly why social change is so slow in our society, how we can make a real difference right now, and why is essential that we do actually start right now.

POLITICS SLOW SOCIAL CHANGE

Whether we're talking about racial justice, universal health care, or even LGBTQ rights, what we're actually talking about is changing social framework and infrastructure. This can be really hard, given that policymakers are beholden to the will of their constituents, and oftentimes, people don't agree on important topics like this. Let's take as a brief example, the debate around Critical Race Theory (CRT).

You can consider CRT loosely as:

...[The] theory that racism is not merely the product of prejudice, but that racism is embedded in American society and its legal system in order to uphold supremacy of white persons."

Now, granted, this definition comes from Republican Governor Ron DeSantis of Florida, in his 2021 ban of CRT from public schools in Florida. It's not necessarily the only or best definition, but I want to call your attention to this because it give us some sense of how this topic is being debated right now.

Recently, Reuters News conducted an online poll of about 1000 or so Americans, both Republican and Democratic. What they found is that among Democrats 51% opposed banning CRT from public schools. Among Republican participants, 54% supported banning CRT from schools. What this tells us is that this topic, though very important, is essentially being legislated along party lines. And what we see as a result is that predominantly Republican states are successful in banning CRT, whereas those that are majority Democrat or not.

Regardless of your stance on it, the important takeaway, here, is that a top down policy-first approach doesn't work. It can't work, as long as we are split almost right down the middle on important issues. But what if we were able to come at this from a different angle?

PEOPLE HAVE TO CHANGE

Arianna Huffington, the co-founder of Huffington Post once said:

Lasting social change unfolds from the inside out, from the inner to the outer being, from inner to outer realities."

What she's getting at here is that we need to change what's within us if we want to change what's around us. Social justice in my eyes, then, goes hand-in-hand with self-improvement work. Generally, when we're talking about this, there are two types of self-improvement mark that I encourage people to lean into, and support. And they are shadow integration, and Social-Emotional Learning (SEL).

I don't have enough time to elaborate on these, but I know that you can do a ton of research on Google Scholar, at your local library, or even at your university library if you have access. However, I do want to offer a brief highlight as to what each of them is.

Regarding shadow work, Jung explained his theory of the shadow self in 1963 and in many of his writings. You can consider what he's saying is that conscious and unconscious minds are what's at the core of how we think and act. And what we want to do with shadow integration is bring them together to make one mind out of these aspects. In other words, bring what's dark in us to light. Through this process, people are able to uncover their unconscious bias, prejudice, fears, and the roots of any other motivations or actions that they may have.

Now, Social-Emotional Learning is a concept that goes as far back as ancient Greece and Plato. And I know it's a hotly debated topic right now. And I again don't want to dive too deep into what it is. But I want to call your attention to this definition that comes to us from Maurice Elias, a professor of psychology, and the Director of the Social-Emotional Learning Lab at Rutgers University.

He says:

"[SEL] is a process through which we learn how to recognize and manage emotions, **care about others**, make good decisions, **behave ethically and responsibly**, **develop positive relationships**, and avoid negative behaviors."

In other words, it's a method of learning that allows students to become good citizens. Together these two processes, shadow integration and SEL, allow individuals to become aware of their positioning within society, to challenge their personal beliefs, and expand their perspectives on social issues, to cultivate empathy towards others and their needs to be inspired to act in support of social justice.

IMAGINE THIS...

Now, I know I've thrown a lot at you, and I don't expect a lot of it to stick right now. In fact, I encourage you to do more research. But I do you want to paint a brief picture to help you envision why this is so important right now.

Imagine for a moment that your sister is arrested, yes, arrested in what should have been a routine traffic stop. And three days later, she's dead in a jail cell.

Imagine your parents struggling, fighting with a curable disease because they can't afford health care.

Imagine your best friend pinned to the ground, begging for breath, because of the color of their skin, their family name or country of origin, or their gender identity. And your pleas for justice and for change? Those are reduced to a "political agenda." Wouldn't you want someone to understand your point of view? Wouldn't you hope that someone out there listening would give you an ear and a little bit of compassion.

Now, I understand that this type of work can be complicated. That it can be tricky. That it can be uncomfortable. But social change is a societal and personal problem that we all have to engage with. We can't ignore it because we all live in a society, and we all support whatever systems are in place by implicitly accepting them.

Even if it's uncomfortable, I highly recommend that you start now. You can do so by reading books like mine, or any of these on this list:

- Bridges to Heal US by Erin Jones
- Caste: The Origins of Our Discontents by Isabel Wilkerson
- Robert A Johnson's Owning Your Own Shadow

And [there are] so many others that are designed to help you to challenge your current beliefs and face this personal work without judgment.

Whether I dress like this...

...or like this...

...my life is not a political agenda.

View/Listen on YouTube

Notes

3. A Better Way

1. Hodges, Sara & Myers, M.W.. (2007). *Encyclopedia of Social Psychology*. Empathy. 296-298.

4. How Did We Get Here?

1. Another valuable piece of history that I never learned was the role of African Americans in sports such as Tommie Smith and John Carlos, two Olympians who raised their fists on the medal podium and had their victories overturned for "unsportsmanlike conduct."

6. Talking about Privilege

1. This is meant as an example of how we all make snap judgements about each other. We all engage in stereotyping. It is not exclusive to one group of people.

7. Getting to the Core of the Problem

1. Smith, Jane Ma'ati, Hermes Trismegistus, and Three Initiates Smith. 2008. *The Emerald Tablet Of Hermes And The Kybalion*. 1st ed. [California]: Independent Publisher.
2. Freud, Sigmund, and Graham Frankland. 2005. *The Unconscious*. London [etc.]: Penguin Books.
3. Johnson, R. A. (1994). *Owning Your Own Shadow: Understanding the Dark Side of the Psyche* (Reprint ed.). HarperSanFrancisco.

8. The Illusion of Separation

1. Also called "othering." It is a process by which people develop their identity at personal and social levels. At the social level, this often creates framing via in-group/out-group dynamics. You can do further reading at https://www.otheringandbelonging.org/the-problem-of-othering/
2. A great starting point would be this article from Britannica's online Encyclopedia: https://www.britannica.com/biography/Musa-I-of-Mali

3. This publication may be challenging to find; however you can gain access through Google Books here: https://books.google.com/books?id=_yIo AAAAYAAJ&printsec=frontcover&source=gbs_ge_summary_r&cad=0#v= onepage&q&f=false

Appendix 1

1. Christian Keysers and Valeria Gazzola, "Hebbian Learning and Predictive Mirror Neurons for Actions, Sensations and Emotions," Philosophical transactions of the Royal Society of London. Series B, Biological sciences (The Royal Society, April 28, 2014), https://www.ncbi.nlm.nih.gov/pmc/articles/ PMC4006178/.
2. Robert barkman, "Why The Human Brain Is So Good At Detecting Patterns", *Psychology Today*, 2022, https://www.psychologytoday.com/us/blog/ singular-perspective/202105/why-the-human-brain-is-so-good-detecting-patterns.
3. Collins, Suzanne. *The Hunger Games*. (New York, NY: Scholastic, 2008) 45.
4. Read more here: https://dqydj.com/baader-meinhof-phenomenon-frequency-bias/
5. This definition comes from Dr. Kee Warner of the University of Colorado at Colorado Springs. He is a sociologist who teaches a class called Communities and the Global Environment to analyze the form, typology, and function of communities and the processes of community development.
6. Available on Amazon and other major online retailers. Lanier also makes an appearance in the 2020 Netflix documentary *The Social Dilemma*, covering the same topic.
7. According to a 2021 Pew Research study, most people who identify as Republican or Conservative distrust the mainstream media as a valid source of news, whereas a majority of Democrats have increased trust in the media. Much of the drop came after President Trump's claims of fake news. This has created a phenomenon where being anti-media has become a part of the GOP identity.

Thank You

The biggest determiners of the future are the choices we make today. In reading this book, you've made the choice to do something to change the course of our future for the better. For that, I want to offer you one last, sincere, "Thank you."

For your bravery.

For your willingness.

For your compassion.

To stand up for what you believe is right, even when it may be unclear or controversial is a show of character that must be acknowledged. You are a leader.

For More Training

If you are a community leader, educator, business owner or nonprofit who would like to learn more about what you can do to bring equity to your organization or looking to set up a training, I invite you to contact my friend and fellow author, Erin Jones.

Erin is a nationally recognized educator, speaker, and trainer and the author of *Bridges to Heal US: Stories and Strategies for Racial Healing.* Below is her contact information so that you can get in touch with me and watch out for more content and free resources as they become available.

Contact

Email: erin@erinjonesdreams.com (for assistant: ty@erin-jonesdreams.com)
Facebook: Erin Jones 2016
Instagram: erinin2016
Twitter: @erinjonesin2016
LinkedIn: http://linkedin.com/in/erin-jones-8a24a814

Acknowledgments

Looking back over this book's first year of life, I have a lot to be thankful for. Above all, I am grateful to all of the people who have supported this book and its message.

To those of you who have read, reviewed, and shared my work. Thank you. You are too numerous to list, but I see you.

To my family, who have provided love, encouragement, and strength in the writing and promotion of this book. You all know better than most how hard it is to put myself out there with a book like this. Thank you for encouraging me to remember my needs.

To my editors and designers, thank you for seeing my vision and helping me bring it to life. Without you, this book couldn't be.

To Erin Jones, *Thank You* for being an inspiration and living the path you set for us. Meeting you has transformed me in so many ways and given me the confidence to stand behind this book the way I couldn't before.

To my Illuminated Authors, you all show me every day what it means to have courage, and I'm honored to be among you as a community leader. Keep bringing light in your own special ways.

ABOUT THE AUTHOR

From part-time writer and editor to bestselling author and book writing coach, Andrae D. Smith, Jr. is the founder of Illuminated Authors writing program.

As a personal-development writer, certified meditation guide, and member of the Natural Healer Society, he is passionate about helping his readers overcome real-world challenges. He seeks to spread empowerment through self-knowledge and compassion in his writings.

After a fateful car accident in 2019 persuaded him to leave a demoralizing retail job, he chose to use his talents full-time and build a new, purpose-driven life. He now devotes his skills and passion to helping inspired entrepreneurs, speakers, and movement leaders write high-impact, value-driven books that transform lives.

Andrae is the author of bestselling book, *Facing Racism* (2020), and "Write Your Book in No Time" (2021)—both of which were written in less than thirty days.

In addition to editing nearly seventy books, he is an Executive Contributor for Brainz Magazine, and has been featured in smaller publications.

When he's not writing or editing, Andrae enjoys learning to play the piano, collecting books (a very different hobby than reading), and enjoying time with his sisters and niece.

facebook.com/AuthorAndrae

instagram.com/author.andraesmith